Making School Count

Promoting urban student motivation and success

Karen Manheim Teel
and
Andrea DeBruin-Parecki

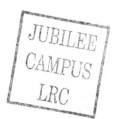

London and New York

First published 2001 by RoutledgeFalmer
11 New Fetter Lane, London EC4P 4EE

Simultaneously published in the USA and Canada
by RoutledgeFalmer
29 West 35th Street, New York, NY 10001

RoutledgeFalmer is an imprint of the Taylor & Francis Group

Typeset in Sabon by Taylor & Francis Books Ltd
Printed and bound in Great Britain by TJ International Ltd,
Padstow, Cornwall

British Library Cataloguing in Publication Data
A catalogue record for this book is available from the British Library

Library of Congress Cataloging in Publication Data
Teel, Karen Manheim
Making school count: promoting urban student motivation and success/
Karen Manheim Teel and Andrea DeBruin-Parecki.
Includes bibliographical references and index.
1. Afro-American students – Education – case studies.
2. Motivation in education – United States – case studies.
3. Educational innovations – United States – case studies.
4. Action research in education – United States – case studies.
I. DeBruin-Parecki, Andrea. II. Title.
LC2717.T44 2000
371.829'96073 – dc21   00–032179

ISBN 0–415–23054–3 (hbk)
ISBN 0–415–23055–1 (pbk)

Karen and Andrea dedicate this book to all the bright, capable, inner-city, African American students who have been considered to be "low achievers," not because of inferior ability, but because of the nature of our public school system in the United States. It is our hope that from this four-year study educators will develop a new perspective on the abilities, talents, and potential of these students and will put that new perspective into action in their schools.

Contents

Foreword

Making School Count is not an abstract book. It is a personal chronicle authored by two gifted teachers – Karen Manheim Teel, a middle school teacher and Andrea DeBruin-Parecki, a university instructor – who believe deeply in the potential of children, who have spent most of their professional lives exploring ways to make manifest that potential, and who have been compelled by the events described here to rethink virtually everything they were ever taught about teaching. Their story involves a decade-long (1989 to present) collaborative struggle to identify and implement instructional strategies in Karen's classroom that are sensitive to the particular needs of disenfranchised students of color as well as the needs of their teachers. I was fortunate enough to be part of this work from the outset.

There is much to recommend *Making School Count*. First, it provides a vivid portrayal of the intersecting lives of school children in the contemporary world of inner-city schools – the jumble of individuals and events, surprises, triumphs, and setbacks that make up the journey on which Karen and Andrea have embarked. This is a world where all of Karen's students wanted to succeed, and many did, but some fell short despite their good intentions and the exciting innovations that Karen brought to the classroom. This is a world where the key to success is the motivations that often lie hidden in the complexities of each individual student's life. Ultimately, Karen discovered that this key for all of her students required a multi-faceted perspective on motivation and an appreciation for its many parts. Some students entered Karen's classroom fully motivated with all the parts in place, while others needed additional rationales for trying hard, and extra support, before they were willing to work up to their potential.

Second, *Making School Count* gives voice to those dedicated, innovative teachers everywhere who are inspired to produce effective change for the benefit of children, often without consideration for the personal and professional toll that such changes can take.

Especially important here is the record of the daily challenges faced by White teachers like Karen who work with students of color from the economically disadvantaged communities in America and who, in the beginning, feel unprepared to work with them.

Third, as a case study, *Making School Count* provides guidance for how teachers can conduct their own action research as a means of improving their teaching and how to create educational change from the "bottom up," one classroom at a time, not "top down," through administrative decree from the superintendent's office.

Fourth, *Making School Count* also illustrates the indispensable role of theory and of empirically derived principles of behavior for guiding and sustaining effective change. It proves anew, page by page, the old adage, "There is nothing as practical as a good theory." There are so many conflicting events, distractions, and puzzling student behaviors that ceaselessly crowd in on teachers that any attempts to deal with each issue individually in isolation from the whole can be overwhelming. Fortunately, good theories draw disparate events into a larger more coherent meaning. Yet, at the same time, events can also challenge theories and cause observers to rethink their original premises or to consider a realignment of possibilities. These dynamics are also part of Karen's and Andrea's story.

Overall, *Making School Count* illustrates how psychological research can best serve education – by offering theoretically derived perspectives and insights to teachers, but only at the invitation of teachers. The matter of invitation is central – just who invites whom? Part of the problem facing responsible school change is that for years experts have all too often invited themselves into the classroom, not as supplicants to learn, or even as guests, but to use classes as laboratories to pursue answers to questions which teachers may see as arcane, distant, and often totally divorced from the practical realities of schooling.

Ideally, the notion of teacher as researcher should involve a collaboration between classroom teachers and university personnel in which they interpret classroom life in theoretical terms with the result that practical, effective strategies for change emerge. *Making School Count* provides a unique testimonial to the benefits of this process.

On a personal note, this work has had a strong impact on my own thinking and teaching practice in my dual role as both an educational theorist and a university professor. For example, Karen's discovery of the "grade aspiration dilemma" – which led her to introduce college and career aspirations as an additional motivator for those of her students who were still lagging behind – has made me appreciate the motivational benefits of linking high achievement in the minds of students in their early years with college and career opportunities in the future – as Karen did. My students at the university are clearly aware of the importance of doing their best as indicated by their academic success, but many younger students lack that awareness which is so critical. In addition, I have become convinced of the importance of field-based, action research not only at the middle school level but at all levels of schooling including colleges and universities. Finally, my own teaching has changed dramatically because of experiences in Karen's classroom where, for example, I came to recognize fully the motivational value to students of assessing their progress against absolute, merit-based standards – where anyone can succeed as long as they live up to the quality and quantity of work demanded by the teacher, instead of measuring themselves competitively against the performance of others.

I am honored to have been a part of the journey undertaken by Karen and Andrea. The experience has increased immeasurably my respect for teachers and my appreciation for the truly daunting tasks that often face them. For me, it has been a time of great professional growth. I now invite you to share in this experience.

Professor Martin V. Covington
University of California, Berkeley

Acknowledgements

We extend special thanks to the following people:

To Karen's students during all four years of this study for their patience and invaluable feedback.

To the authors of the literature we read, describing the enormous but untapped potential of African American students – for their inspiration and insight.

To Dr. Martin V. Covington and the graduate students at the University of California at Berkeley who participated in this study as curriculum designers, participant observers, teachers, and researchers.

To the teachers, administrators, and support personnel at the urban middle school where Karen taught and where we did this research, for their interest and support.

To the Spencer Foundation for supporting this work with a two-year Postdoctoral Fellowship.

To Gail Harrison for her commitment and collaboration as a daily observer in Karen's class for two years.

To Dr. Mary-Lynn Lidstone for her time and excellent suggestions in helping us clearly articulate our ideas.

And especially to our families for always believing in us and being there for us:

To Karen's family: Woody and their children Liane, Katie, and Skip.

To Andrea's family: Mario and their children Emily, Josh, and Larissa.

Chapter 1

Life in an urban classroom
Where dreams and realities collide

> *What stands out for me is the positive rapport that has developed between me and my students at this point. There are moments during class when one or more students are acting silly, flirting, and goofing around, but I can usually redirect their energies. Even with this rapport, though, I continue to be confused about why the students are not getting their work done and turned in and why they don't resubmit their work with corrections. I know they want A's but something is getting in their way. I wonder if they know what it is.*
>
> (Karen's Journal, 12/1/95)

The notes above were the reflections of the first author of this book, Karen Teel, as she pondered her predominantly African American, inner-city students' behavior in her eighth grade US History class and how she could convince them to do their very best, thereby *making school count*. As she says in these notes, there are clearly many forces at work, often elusive to teachers (and maybe to the students themselves), which undermine student motivation and learning and which determine student "achievement" in school.

In an attempt to understand better those elusive forces and to discover the keys to high achievement for this student population, a four-year classroom study was undertaken (1990–2 and 1994–6). Our book is based on that study, during which Karen used and collaboratively evaluated alternative teaching strategies designed to honor and motivate "low-achieving," inner-city, African American middle school students. When we use the term "low-achieving" or "low achievement" in this book, we are referring to low academic success as determined by teacher evaluations, grades received, and test scores. We put quotes around these labels because we believe that those students who are considered to be "low-achieving" – based on traditional teaching criteria for success and standardized tests – are often very capable but are not typically allowed to demonstrate their individual skills and talents.

How our book began

Because of our beliefs about the biases inherent in traditional teaching strategies and evaluation criteria, in 1989, the authors of this book, along with professors and graduate students – many of whom were classroom teachers – came together in a graduate seminar at the University of California at Berkeley. The seminar was organized by Dr. Martin Covington, a psychology professor specializing in achievement motivation theory, and by the first author, Karen Teel (referred to as Karen by the authors of the book and as Mrs. Teel by interviewers and her students), who was an experienced classroom teacher and a doctoral student in education. Second author Andrea DeBruin-Parecki (referred to as Andrea by the authors of the book) was a participant in this unique university seminar and became a collaborating classroom researcher and data analyst.

Literature regarding the education of African American students makes it clear that in American public schools these students often do not have the same academic success rate as their Caucasian counterparts (Boykin, 1994; Cummins, 1986; Delpit, 1995; Graham, 1994; Haberman, 1991; Hale, 1994; Heath, 1983; Irvine, 1990; Knapp et al., 1992; Ladson-Billings, 1994; Lomotey, 1990; Ogbu and Matute-Bianchi, 1986; US Census and Bureau of Labor Statistics, 1997). Over the years, as visitors and/or classroom teachers, all the seminar participants had observed large numbers of bright, capable, and enthusiastic inner-city, African American students in elementary schools. Because of those positive experiences, we were concerned about what happens to these students who show so much promise in elementary school yet often do poorly in junior high and high school. We were all familiar with various theories, described below, which discuss the disproportionate "low achievement" of these students.

Some educators attribute the "low achievement" of inner-city African American students, in part, to the social, economic, psychological, and environmental disadvantages of poverty, including its effects on family life and structure (Bowles and Gintis, 1986; Coleman, 1966; Jencks *et al.*, 1972). Others blame the assessment criteria used in the early years of elementary school (Heath, 1983; Marshall and Weinstein, 1984). There are also educators who attribute the "low achievement" in school of these students to disempowerment caused by a history of discrimination as African Americans in the United States, and to the emphasis on a Eurocentric curriculum throughout the elementary and secondary school years (Cummins, 1986; Hilliard, 1978; Ogbu and Matute-Bianchi, 1986; Rashid, 1981). The Eurocentric curriculum considers Europe and Europeans central to world culture, history, and economics.

The seminar participants rejected any theories that blamed the students and/or their families for their "low achievement." Instead, we concurred that there must be a typical pattern in public schools in which the strengths, talents, and culture of inner-city, African American students are neither acknowledged in curriculum design and practice nor validated in the evaluation of their school work (Bernstein, 1977; Bourdieu, 1977; Cummins, 1986; Heath, 1983; Hilliard, 1978; MacLeod, 1987; Marshall and Weinstein, 1984, 1986; Ogbu and Matute-Bianchi, 1986). MacLeod describes this phenomenon in *Ain't no makin' it* (1987: 99):

> The problem is not that lower-class children are inferior in some way; the problem is that *by the definitions and standards of the school*, they consistently are evaluated as deficient.

Our purpose in the seminar was to collaboratively design a more academically and culturally supportive classroom environment for Karen's students. We decided to develop teaching strategies that would substitute for the inappropriate strategies we had read about in the literature and had observed first-hand in schools. Examples of those inappropriate strategies are: a reliance on reading as the sole source of information, an emphasis on formal writing skills to the exclusion of other ways of demonstrating knowledge, such as through skits, models, oral presentations, or artwork, and the prevalent use of a Eurocentric curriculum with little or no recognition given to the histories and contributions of other cultures.

The seminar participants did not believe that teachers intentionally used inappropriate strategies and curricula. Instead, we agreed that many of them simply were not sufficiently familiar with the differences in backgrounds, cultures, and academic strengths and weaknesses between these students and middle-class Caucasian students (Delpit, 1995; Diller, 1999; Ladson-Billings, 1994; Obidah and Teel, 1996, 2001; Sleeter, 1994). Our view is that when such culturally inappropriate strategies are used, they discourage these students from reaching their full potential, often alienating them from school (Giroux, 1983; Ogbu, 1987).

Based on our convictions outlined above, our main focus at the outset of the seminar was on designing alternatives to the types of culturally inappropriate teaching strategies described earlier. We believed that these alternative strategies would promote higher achievement (i.e. A's and B's) among Karen's African American middle school students because the strategies would be academically and culturally compatible with the students while at the same time require high performance standards. The alternative strategies we designed were: a non-competitive classroom structure with effort-based grading, multiple performance opportunities, increased student responsibility and choice, and validation of cultural heritage (Teel et al., 1994, 1998).

Our four-year classroom study

Following the seminar, as had been initially planned, Karen returned to her school district (after a four-year leave) where she became both a seventh grade World History teacher and a teacher researcher in an urban middle school (Cochran-Smith and Lytle, 1990, 1993; Hollingsworth et al., 1994). Having an experienced middle school teacher in the classroom every day, acting as a teacher researcher during our study, made it possible to examine more closely the students' responses to our alternative teaching strategies. Karen also arranged for an assisting observer to visit the classroom twice a week the first two years and daily the third and fourth years.

For four years (1990–2 and 1994–6), Karen used the alternative teaching strategies mentioned earlier to promote the success of all students who satisfied her performance expectations. Those expectations were clearly connected to the required curricula, were rigorous, and were precisely outlined for the students. This alternative approach shifted the grading climate from an "ability game" to an "equity game" in which hard work, persistence, and self-improvement were reinforced (Covington and Teel, 1996). In each of Karen's classes, most of the students were African American. However, there were also a small number of Asian, Caucasian, and Hispanic students. While our study focused on the African American students in the class, we felt that the alternative teaching strategies Karen used would be beneficial to all of our students.

During the first year, Andrea came into Karen's classroom twice a week to observe and to keep a running narrative of the classroom experiences which she summarized regularly. From the start of this research, we worked together to develop a clear, comprehensive coding system to determine the impact of our strategies on student motivation and achievement. In the second year, Andrea became a data analyst for our study, since she had moved across the country to the University of Michigan to start graduate school. A graduate student from the University of California at Berkeley became the assisting observer in Karen's classroom during that second year.

At the end of the first two years (1990–2), our data revealed that the majority of Karen's previously "low-achieving" African American students improved their academic motivation and performance compared to the beginning of the year and compared with their other classes. Some of the students who improved received "A's" and "B's," while others received "C's". However, even though most of the students' grades improved by the end of the first two years of our study, new questions emerged from our data.

For example, during the first and second years of the study, some of the comments students made in private conversations and during class discussions about the significance of their improved grades led us to wonder what the actual impact of the higher grades was on the students' academic self-confidence. We define academic self-confidence as student persistence in their work because they have trust in their ability to succeed. We had noted that some of the students described the class as "easy." We were not certain of their definition of "easy" and whether or not such a view of the class lessened their pride in their grade which would affect any change in their academic self-confidence.

Also, we were puzzled as to why some students continued to receive "C's", "D's", and "F's" when Karen had high expectations for their performance, they said they wanted top grades, and they also had many opportunities to improve their work. We speculated as to possible obstacles that might be getting in the way of the motivation and hard work necessary to earn "A's" and "B's" for the students receiving the lower grades.

Following those first two years of our research, in an attempt to study more closely the impact of our alternative teaching strategies – both successful ("A's" and "B's") and unsuccessful ("C's" and below) – our most recent classroom research was undertaken (1994–6). The discovery of unexpected obstacles to high achievement during those first two years led to this second phase of our research which was more about factors which might prevent improved student self-confidence and about additional obstacles to student high achievement (Chapter 7).

The third- and fourth-year research was funded by a two-year Spencer Postdoctoral Fellowship awarded to Karen. We studied factors that might prevent stronger academic self-confidence. These factors were: (1) our students' belief that they received good grades due to easy work rather than to their ability (Weiner, 1977), and (2) the large number of high grades in the class which might lessen their value. We also considered obstacles to "high achievement" such as the students' potential discomfort with higher grades because of peer pressure (Fordham and Ogbu, 1986) and the expressed willingness of some of them to accept "C's" and "D's" even when they had many opportunities to raise their grades on each assignment.

In addition, during the third and fourth years of our research, Karen taught a new group of predominantly African American inner-city students. Specifically, in the third year, these students were in seventh grade World History. During the fourth year, approximately half of these same seventh graders returned for Karen's eighth grade US History class. Attrition rates and class schedules did not allow all the original group of students to remain intact for the two years.

The heart of this book is the story and analysis of evolving student attitudes and behaviors as they responded to the alternative curricula and grading approaches Karen used over the course of our work. The story will be told by the students themselves, by Karen as their history teacher, by the assisting observers, and by Andrea who, during the third and fourth years of the study, had become a professor of education at the University of Northern Iowa.

During all four years of the study, both Karen and Andrea reviewed all of the classroom observation write-ups as well as interview and questionnaire data so that interrater reliability would be built into the study. During each of the four years, Karen modified her teaching approach from time to time in response to student feedback, observer feedback, and feedback from Andrea (Bullough Jr. and Gitlin, 1995; Mills, 2000).

Four facets of the book

This book is unique in the four interlocking facets that it embodies. First and foremost, it represents the authors' *dual conviction* about culturally appropriate teaching strategies. The first conviction is that the disproportionate "low achievement" of inner-city African American students is partly the result of teaching strategies used by many teachers that are culturally inappropriate (Cummins, 1986; Delpit, 1995; Hilliard, 1978; Ladson-Billings, 1994; Lomotey, 1990; MacLeod, 1987; Marshall and Weinstein, 1984, 1986; Weinstein, 1989). Our second conviction is that Caucasian teachers – who currently form the majority of professionals dealing with minority students – should be involved in making the changes that will address this achievement problem. This challenge to Caucasian teachers is considerable given the fact that so many are not prepared to work effectively with students of color (Delpit, 1995; Diller, 1999; Ladson-Billings, 1994; Obidah and Teel, 1996, 2001; Sleeter, 1994).

Second, our book is a *narrative* (Connelly and Clandinin, 1987, 1990) – the story of how we addressed our two convictions in a single classroom during four different years. Karen (who is Caucasian) faced cross-cultural challenges with her inner-city, African American students in an attempt to improve the motivational and learning climate of her classroom. In a larger sense, our narrative captures the dreams and the realities in an urban classroom, including triumphs, surprises, and inevitable setbacks that accompany any serious attempts at educational change.

Third, our book serves as a *case study* of a collaborative model, harnessing the resources of a university and of a school, attempting to bring about educational change from the ground up, one class at a time.

Fourth, the book is meant to be a *resource* for all teachers who aspire to become innovators and researchers for change in their own classrooms. It will clarify what it means to conduct classroom-based, action research (Bullough Jr. and Gitlin, 1995; Mills, 2000), the role of theory in guiding classroom strategies for change, and how to evaluate the impact of change.

Organization of the book

The book is organized into nine chapters, with the introduction as Chapter 1. In Chapter 2 Karen tells her story of becoming a teacher researcher. In Chapter 3, we outline our theoretical framework and the substance of the alternative teaching strategies we designed in the graduate seminar. Chapter 4 presents the context in which the study took place, highlighting the school, the teachers, and the students. Chapter 5 discusses the teacher action research process used in this study for recognizing problems, collecting and analyzing data, and making classroom adjustments accordingly. Chapter 6 describes the impact of the alternative teaching strategies on the students' motivation and success. Chapter 7 reviews possible obstacles to our students' success, including the "grade aspiration dilemma" that we discovered during the study. Chapter 8 relates Karen's responses to the obstacles, including the stages she went through in trying to address the obstacles and student reactions to her efforts. In Chapter 8, we also discuss the idea of connecting the students' college and career aspirations to teaching strategies and to student performance in class. Finally, Chapter 9 includes suggestions for turning student aspirations into reality through changes in teaching and teacher education.

Chapter 2

The personal journey of a teacher

Karen's story

Neither interpretive nor process-product classroom research has foregrounded the teacher's role in the generation of knowledge about teaching. What is missing from the knowledge base for teaching, therefore, are the voices of the teachers themselves, the questions teachers ask, the ways teachers use writing and intentional talk in their work lives, and the interpretive frames teachers use to understand and improve their own classroom practices.

(Cochran-Smith and Lytle, 1990: 2)

I have been a classroom teacher for over thirty years, but in the beginning years of my teaching career I was not, nor did I ever think of being a "teacher researcher." I always knew that my work as a teacher was extremely important and meaningful, but I never thought about documenting the process in any way and sharing my findings with the research community as Cochran-Smith and Lytle suggest above.

As a classroom teacher, I tried to challenge and interest my students with the methods I used. However, I did not seriously investigate my own work in order to understand better its impact on their attitudes, behavior, and performance, which is the suggested teacher role discussed in the most recent literature on teacher research (Anderson *et al.*, 1994; Bullough Jr. and Gitlin, 1995; Cochran-Smith and Lytle, 1990, 1993; Hollingsworth *et al.*, 1994).

In recent years, teacher research has become a recognized mode of inquiry with a potential for yielding rich insights and a legitimate knowledge base for the study of teaching, learning, and the process of education in general. Teachers' classroom experiences, carefully documented, can reveal the complexities inherent in teaching. They can suggest theoretical frameworks about such issues as motivation and learning derived from hours of observations, conversations with students, reflection, and sharing with teachers and others. When classroom teachers think of themselves as teacher researchers, they more closely examine student responses to the classroom experience.

Sociologists of teaching tell us that what many teachers enjoy the most about teaching is the interaction with their students, particularly the relationships they develop with individual students (Bennet, 1985; Lortie, 1975). For me, too, the interactive part of teaching has always been the most meaningful. I have always loved teaching because I enjoy thinking and learning about various topics with others. Below, is an excerpt from my reflections about teaching, written the fourth year of our study.

> *It just occurred to me that even though I love teaching history, what I find the most challenging (and ultimately the most rewarding) about my job is relating to the students on a social level and developing relationships with each of them. I relish the psychological/social aspects of being a teacher. I find these aspects especially challenging because the kids are at such a critical stage in their development as students and as people in general. So much is going on in my students' heads and bodies, and being able to manage all of those forces plus turning my students on to history are very exciting objectives. When it all comes together, I find myself on cloud 9 with an overwhelming feeling of satisfaction and accomplishment. I feel like I've taken on and met the greatest challenge there is in education!!!*
>
> (Karen's Journal, 4/25/96)

I always thought of teaching as stirring my students' curiosities, challenging them to think about various topics, and guiding them in the learning process. I long believed that to be effective a teacher just needed to use the right methods and be a caring person. If my teaching was not going well, I was critical of my methods, and I looked for new and different ways of presenting the subject matter. But, on reflection, I now realize that I never considered my students' backgrounds, personalities, and interests in my curriculum planning.

The first phase of my teaching career in the Foothill School District (all names of districts, schools, and students are fictitious) spanned a fourteen-year period. I taught ten years at the junior high level and four years at the senior high level. The Foothill School District has a diverse student population, including a fairly large African American student population from low-income communities.

During the first ten years of my teaching career, however, I was a teacher at Taylor Junior High School which is in a primarily middle-class, Caucasian, suburban community that is also a part of the Foothill School District. During the years that I taught at Taylor, an increasing percentage of inner-city African American students attended. From 1970 to 1977, the proportion of African American students at Taylor grew from 2 percent to 18 percent. I realized some years later that almost invariably the African American students ended up in the lowest-tracked classes.

During my last two years at Taylor, from 1977 to 1979, at my request, I taught several of the lowest-tracked classes. In retrospect, I must admit that I taught the students in the lowest-tracked classes with very different methods than I used with my higher-tracked classes because I did not have the same high expectations for them. My experience corroborates the research of Marshall and Weinstein (1984, 1986) and of Weinstein (1986, 1991) in which they found that teachers have very different expectations for "low-achieving" students than they do for the more "high-achieving" students. Depending on whether they are elementary or secondary teachers, these expectations are based on the teachers' knowledge of test scores, on previous performance assessments, and sometimes on race, ethnicity, and gender factors.

During these years of teaching, before I started graduate school, I had many enriching, rewarding opportunities to interact with colleagues both in my schools and at district and state-wide functions. For example, I worked on an innovative curriculum with individual teachers in my school and at other schools in my district. I was also a member of district-wide curriculum development and textbook adoption committees. In addition, I regularly attended regional social studies conferences. I always came away from those interactive experiences with new insights, new ideas, and renewed commitment to my profession. During those interactions, I felt important, intelligent, and professional. However, on reflection, I also remained limited in my understanding of my students' attitudes, behavior, abilities, and motivation. Probably like most teachers, during numerous classroom experiences, I found myself confused, disappointed, and angry when various lessons did not go well for some of my students. I rarely blamed the students for poor performance on an assignment; I blamed a flawed lesson plan. I would think of a different way to present the subject matter, but without taking into account who my students were and whether or not they were learning.

My limited feelings of success as a teacher continued. Such perceptions of limited success cause many teachers to leave the classroom permanently. Some pursue new careers while others become school administrators.

Because I was getting more and more frustrated as a classroom teacher, instead of leaving the teaching profession, I decided to go to graduate school at the University of California at Berkeley in search of answers to the numerous questions I had about my teaching and about my students' motivation and learning. I wanted to find theoretical answers to the questions that came from my own practice. I was convinced that, by developing a deeper understanding of some of the basic principles of teaching and learning, I would be in a better position to promote success with my students.

In graduate school, my interest in student motivation and learning turned to African American students in urban schools because that was the student population that my professors focused on. In my classes, I read several books and articles describing theories about the experiences of inner-city African American students in public schools which completely changed my perception of why these students "under-achieve" (Anyon, 1981; Cummins, 1986; Heath, 1983; MacLeod, 1987; Marshall and Weinstein, 1984, 1986; Ogbu and Matute-Bianchi, 1986; Rubin, 1976). I no longer believed that the students and their families were to blame for this problem. Rather, I came to believe that the schools were responsible.

In addition, at this time, I became a research assistant for Dr. Sandra Hollingsworth who was also at the University of California at Berkeley. I worked on a study she had initiated which looked at how beginning teachers learned to teach reading. The study took me into urban classrooms, both elementary and secondary, and gave me opportunities to talk at great length with the teachers and to observe the students in those classrooms (Hollingsworth *et al.*, 1992, 1994).

In a graduate course that I took with Dr. Hollingsworth, she also introduced me to the concept of the teacher as researcher which dramatically influenced my view of the possible roles of teachers in schools. Until my contact with Dr. Hollingsworth and the notion of teacher as researcher, I had always considered myself and other teachers to be practitioners who could only become effective teachers by taking advice from and being guided by scholars in the field of education, and by acquiring ideas from fellow teachers. In other words, I had seen myself as dependent on other educators, believing that the way to find solutions to my problems was to gather information outside my classroom rather than from within.

After four years in graduate school, I had developed a new perspective of myself as a teacher researcher and of the "low achievement" of inner-city African American students. I was determined to develop and use a more culturally appropriate teaching approach than I thought was being used with junior high school classes populated primarily by African American students from low-income communities.

I decided to teach World History because I had ten years experience at the junior high level. In addition to French, I was qualified to teach history according to my standard secondary teaching credential. I also knew from my previous experience that teaching history would allow me the flexibility I needed to try out innovative classroom goal structures, grading systems, teaching strategies, and performance opportunities.

As we mentioned in the introduction, Dr. Martin Covington (1984, 1992, 1998), an achievement motivation theorist in the Psychology Department at the University of California at Berkeley, was also interested in developing and testing non-traditional strategies and curricula in the schools. He suggested that we organize a seminar around my class. I was eager to work together with other university researchers and teachers because of the rich experiences and sense of support that I had had over the years with collaboration. Our work together, discussing and designing alternative teaching strategies, turned into the study on which this book is based.

Chapter 3

Developing teaching strategies that honor and motivate diverse learners

> An equity game involves rewarding the struggle for self-improvement, not winning over others; promoting effort, not aggrandizing ability; and encouraging creativity, not fostering compliance.
>
> (Covington and Teel, 1996: 8)

This chapter describes the theoretical framework supporting our innovative teaching strategies and the teaching strategies themselves. All of our strategies, and the theories on which they were based, were designed to help our students become aware of their talents and of their thinking abilities and to promote the success of all of the students in Karen's classroom. As Covington and Teel describe above, our goal was to create an "equity game" in Karen's classroom.

Over the years many new, interesting, and relevant theoretical perspectives on "low student achievement" have been brought into our work. Those perspectives will be discussed later in the book. It was with the work of the researchers described below, however, that we first began to develop the theoretical framework for our study.

Theoretical framework

Researchers have demonstrated a strong relationship between student attitudes towards school and towards themselves as learners on the one hand, and their achievement motivation and academic success on the other (Anyon, 1981; Brophy, 1987; Covington, 1984; Cummins, 1986; Giroux, 1984; Marshall and Weinstein, 1984; Ogbu and Matute-Bianchi, 1986; Thomas,

1980). The classroom approach described in this book was designed by the authors and their colleagues using the motivation and school failure theories of Covington (1984), Marshall and Weinstein (1984, 1986), Weinstein (1983, 1986), Cummins (1986), and Ogbu and Matute-Bianchi (1986).

Self-worth theory: motives as the protection of personal worth

According to the self-worth theory of achievement motivation (Covington, 1984; Covington and Beery, 1976), a sense of academic self-worth is the most critical factor in determining student attitudes and behavior. The key to academic self-worth is students' perceptions of their own ability in school, especially in comparison with others. Students learn to avoid shame and humiliation due to failure by choosing not to try. This type of intentional, resistant classroom behavior has been coined "negative motivation" (Covington, 1984).

However, by not trying on an assignment, the students risk criticism and possible consequences imposed on them by their teacher and families who expect them to "at least try." This is the "double-edged sword" of the theory (Covington and Omelich, 1979) in which you are viewed as lazy if you do not try, but, at the same time, you are viewed as incompetent if you do try and fail.

Competitive classroom structure

Covington suggests that many disruptive off-task behaviors that teachers must contend with on a daily basis are reactive behaviors (negative motivation). These behaviors result from a history of uncomfortable classroom and/or school-wide experiences during which learning was designated as a narrowly defined "ability game" where there were few winners. These behaviors may have little to do with the current teacher and classroom environment. In order to promote positive student motivation and high achievement, Covington advocates a classroom approach moving away from competition with others to one emphasizing effort and individual mastery learning, with engaging tasks which result in more widespread success through intrinsic motivation. Covington's emphasis on effort over narrowly defined ability was one of the major components contributing to our research design.

Research on differential teacher expectations

Weinstein (1983, 1986) and Marshall and Weinstein (1984, 1986) also focus their research on school failure. Specifically, they have studied discrepancies in student achievement attributed to teacher expectations. Marshall and Weinstein have found that teachers have lower expectations for students identified as "low achievers" based on very limited criteria such as reading and writing skills. For those who are negatively slotted, learning often becomes an exercise in frustration, leading to apathy, poor achievement, and other counterproductive school behaviors and attitudes (Marshall and Weinstein, 1986).

In classrooms where differential treatment occurs less frequently, teachers provide positive feedback to all students in the context of a variety of tasks and mixed-ability group structures. These teachers also have more positive relationships with their students. In these classrooms, students share more responsibility for their own learning and evaluation, and assessment is used as a guide for learning as opposed to a measure of ability and performance.

Weinstein and colleagues have identified a number of inappropriate strategies, stemming from differential teacher expectations, that many teachers are using in classrooms today. The participants in this research project decided to work specifically to correct two of the inappropriate teaching strategies presented in their work: (1) limited performance opportunities and grading criteria; and (2) limited responsibility and choice given to students.

Limited performance opportunities and grading criteria

Typically, in classrooms, there is a limited variety of assignments and activities offered to the students. Those who do well on them become the "high achievers" and those who do poorly become the "low achievers." Grades are usually determined by very limited criteria. For example, reading and writing skills are given most attention in schools, whereas oral and narrative skills, artistic skills, leadership skills, imagination, and creativity are not given the same respect, curricular emphasis, and credit (Heath, 1983, 1986; Phillips, 1972; Rosenholtz, 1979). These limited performance opportunities allow few students to succeed, since different tasks capture different types of intelligence (Rosenholtz and Simpson, 1984). Consequently, those students with the strongest reading and writing skills excel early on in school, develop stronger academic self-esteem than those with weaker reading and writing skills, and typically end up being the "high achievers."

Lack of student empowerment: limited responsibility and choice given to the students

If there are leadership opportunities or occasions when student feedback is solicited, it is normally the "higher achievers" who are called on (Weinstein et al., 1982). This results in unrecognized and underdeveloped talent among those students who have been labeled "low achievers" (Cummins, 1986; Thomas, 1980; Verble, 1985). At the present time in American schools, students have few opportunities to participate in decision-making in relation to the curriculum, and few choices are offered to students when they are given assignments (Covington, 1984).

Issues particular to African American students

Covington, Marshall and Weinstein, and Weinstein all address the problem of school failure for all students considered at risk. Because this study focused on "low-achieving," inner-city African American students, school-failure literature specific to their culture was also explored. Much of that literature centers around notions of Eurocentric curricula and identity crises.

Eurocentric curricula

Schools and teachers have traditionally failed to honor African American heritage and culture by not acknowledging multiple perspectives and diverse cultures in the curriculum and instruction (Cummins, 1986; Delpit, 1988; Graham, 1988; Hale-Benson, 1990; Irvine, 1990). This approach has often alienated students rather than supported them through validation of their cultural heritage. On the other hand, Caucasian students have experienced cultural validation over the years because European culture has been the traditional focus in American schools.

Identity crisis

According to a number of studies, many African American high school students have created a type of "counter-culture" to protect their sense of identity as a way of coping with racial discrimination and the devaluing of their cultural heritage in the classroom (Ogbu and Matute-Bianchi, 1986). Inner-city, African American students often struggle between representing their own cultural norms or conforming to mainstream standards. As a part of this conflict, students often resist doing well in a competitive structure for a variety of reasons including the stigma of "acting white" (Fordham and Ogbu, 1986). This attitude often reveals itself in the form of negative motivation.

Alternative teaching strategies

Based on the motivation and school-failure theories described above, we designed four alternative teaching strategies to put into practice in Karen's classroom. The four strategies were: (1) a non-competitive classroom structure with effort-based grading; (2) multiple performance opportunities; (3) increased student responsibility and choice; and (4) validation of cultural heritage. By incorporating these four strategies into the curriculum, assessment, and instruction, our goal was to promote higher levels of motivation, achievement, and learning by recognizing and honoring the students' diverse learning styles, strengths, talents, and interests.

A non-competitive classroom structure with effort-based grading

Based on Covington's self-worth theory of achievement motivation (1984) and on Marshall and Weinstein's view about the detrimental effects of differential teacher expectations (1984, 1986), we designed a non-competitive, effort-based grading system. If we believe that success in school is a key to academic self-esteem, then those students who fail in a competitive classroom structure – where only a limited number of students can succeed – will probably develop low academic self-esteem.

Specifically, in an attempt to change this outcome, a new environment was created in Karen's classroom, in which individual effort and group cooperation were encouraged, rather than competition and a "win/lose" scenario. Lessons were developed which students could complete successfully either the first time – if they met the standards expected by the teacher – or after they revised their work using the teacher's feedback to improve. Effort and improvement were stressed because the participants wanted to give the students every opportunity to learn from the assignments and to earn a good grade. Grades were determined on an individual basis, not on a comparative basis, taking into consideration cooperation, participation, effort, and quality of work.

To be sure that her students understood that effort was the key criteria for success in Karen's class, she always encouraged them to try hard, and recognized them when they did. She was also consistent in her remarks about second chances. She let them know that she understood there were times that they would not be able to turn an assignment in on time. She augmented that statement by telling them that if they were willing to turn assignments in late, they would be accepted with a small penalty. This penalty was usually lowering a student's grade by one grade level unless the student had an excellent excuse. In time, it became clear to the students that losing some credit was far better than losing it all.

The grading system was designed to assist adolescents in developing stronger images of themselves as students. Individual improvement was emphasized rather than comparison with others on a class-wide basis. The students always knew where they stood in Karen's class, since they kept track of their own grades. There was little excuse for being surprised by an unexpected grade. In addition, by knowing what grade they had earned at any given time, they could speak with Karen about discrepancies and/or problems. The large variety of tasks and assignments given to students each quarter also assisted students in raising their grades. As discussed in the next section, there were always activities that sparked their interest and motivated them to do well.

Multiple performance opportunities

Another goal of our approach was to recognize and honor student interest, strengths, and talents by providing them with a variety of assignments as opposed to assignments which only emphasized reading and writing skills. This goal was consistent with what

Marshall and Weinstein were advocating (Marshall and Weinstein, 1984, 1986).

Students were given opportunities to demonstrate their imagination and creativity through varied means including the use of oral, narrative, and artistic skills along with the more traditional reading and writing skills. Some examples of the diverse activities made available to the students were skits, worksheets, quizzes, tests, oral presentations, book talks, art projects, simulation games, map work, computer projects, note-taking, reading sessions, and group work. These activities required leadership, planning, creative writing, and artwork on the part of the students. Hence, the students' final quarter grades were based on a wide variety of activities which put academic success within their reach (Marshall and Weinstein, 1984; Rosenholtz and Simpson, 1984).

One of the activities we designed for the students was preparing and presenting skits in class. For example, as the culminating activity of the unit on Ancient Rome in the first year, the students planned and presented skits representing different causes of Rome's collapse. One group represented the army, another the unemployed, another the family. After gathering some information about the circumstances these people found themselves in toward the final years of the Roman Empire, the students incorporated what they had learned into short skits. Most groups organized costumes and props as well. The group who portrayed the Roman army set up their skit as if they were soldiers huddled around a campfire far away from Rome, in one of the provinces. They talked about attacks on Rome by groups coming in from outside the Roman Empire, and about corruption among the Roman army officers. Within this context, the students explained why soldiers thought Rome fell. They were graded on a number of aspects including creativity, content, and ability to answer questions posed by the class. This type of task challenged students to use a variety of their strengths and talents, and, according to our data, they learned the content as well.

Increased student responsibility and choice

In response to the concerns of Marshall and Weinstein (1984, 1986), Karen furnished the students with more responsibilities than teachers typically offer students. For example, students were given leadership opportunities in the classroom on a regular, voluntary basis as classroom officers. Some of their duties included: passing out and collecting needed materials, running errands, and setting up video equipment. The tasks were small, but they helped to create a sense of community, ownership, and responsibility in Karen's classroom.

Karen also gave the students many assignment choices in order to provide students with even more of a feeling of ownership of the classroom. She empowered the students by allowing them to assist her in making curriculum decisions such as which aspects of a culture they wanted to study. Students were always given choices of books to read during silent reading time, as well as choices of assignments whenever feasible. We believed that by giving students more responsibility and choice along with opportunities to influence the teacher's curriculum decisions they would begin to develop a sense of authority in the classroom, and this would reduce their resistance to the teacher's agenda (Thomas, 1980).

Validation of cultural heritage

Working toward validating cultural heritage was clearly one of our high priorities because of the prevalence in schools of a Eurocentric curriculum (Cummins, 1986; Ogbu and Matute-Bianchi, 1986). As we searched for ways to accomplish this, a direction came to us from the students when the first cohort initially went to the school library. Most of the students selected biographies and historical fiction from their own cultural backgrounds. Inspired by the students' interest in these types of stories, Karen put together a classroom library of historical fiction and biographies which represented all of the students' cultural backgrounds. Thus, the classroom library consisted of African American, Asian, Caucasian, Hispanic, and Native American literature. The students read a book of their choice three times a week for 10 minutes of class time. Each week, volunteers were given the opportunity to share self-selected highlights of their books. Those student presentations became known as "book talks." Frequently, race relations was a topic raised by the students in reference to their books.

As a means of addressing the "identity crisis" (the need for African Americans to protect their cultural identity) that Ogbu and Matute-Bianchi (1986) have written about, Karen set aside time on a weekly basis to discuss topics relevant to the students' lives. Current events were discussed on a regular basis, and, whenever there were particular news stories students were interested in, they became a topic of conversation. On occasion, the discussion became very heated. Many students expressed anger and resentment about articles they had read that contained elements of racism such as those about the Ku Klux Klan. Karen tried her best to recognize and validate the students' concerns and encourage them to pose possible solutions. Based on participation levels and critical discussions that resulted from reading or hearing about these articles, students appeared to appreciate these opportunities to share their fears, anger, and doubts.

Ongoing adjustments

As the project progressed, the researchers in this study decided to modify the teaching and grading strategies according to student responses (Mills, 2000). When strategies appeared to be working well as measured by student motivation and engagement, the principles underlying the strategies were incorporated into the curriculum on a wider scale. For example, toward the end of the second year, the participants in the research project designed a unit about a number of different cultures during the Middle Ages, incorporating multiple performance opportunities and choice into the requirements for the project. The students worked in groups, and each member of the group had some choice on what their topics would be and how they would represent the information they gathered about it. The students responded very positively to the way this project was structured. Here is an excerpt from Karen's journal regarding this project:

> *This project on the six cultures was the best one we did all year, I think. The students seemed to like it, judging by their engagement and enthusiasm, and I think they learned a lot, based on their test answers and discussions we had. The group members worked well together because they each were responsible for two topics, and they all had to contribute to putting the booklet together with illustrations and a cover.*
>
> (Karen's Journal, 6/8/92)

When strategies did not work as measured by student apathy and/or disruption, the researchers made decisions about what was causing the poor responses – especially based on student feedback. Karen did not repeat those strategies, or they were revised and then repeated. As one example, our initial attempts to encourage multiple ways of expressing student knowledge involved providing several choices from which students were to select one task to work on. Unfortunately, because these youngsters were so unaccustomed to academic decision-making (according to student self-report), many of them had difficulties dealing with choice. Some students even declined to decide in the face of choice, and worked on something else or became disruptive, while others picked the simplest or easiest task, irrespective of their strongest skills, which defeated our original intention.

A modified, alternative strategy proved much more effective. Instead of offering choices within assignments, we started to vary the types of assignments required – without any choices – so that the students had the opportunity to use their diverse strengths and talents on some of the assignments and to work on their weaker skills on others. Even though this particular example of providing the students with choice did not work out, we still believed that offering the students some choices in their classroom experience was important. Karen continued to ask their opinion about what aspects of a culture they wanted to study and to offer them many choices of books to read during their silent reading time. The examples above represent the ways in which curriculum and grading strategies used over the four years of this study evolved according to student response.

In Chapter 6, strategies will be more carefully explained in the context of instruction, and student and teacher responses will be given in their own voices via interviews, open-ended survey questions, journal writings, and detailed notes from observations. Our data analysis will show the results of linking our theoretical ideas to Karen's classroom teaching strategies. In the next chapter, we describe the context of our study, highlighting the school environment, the teachers, and the students.

Chapter 4

The culture of the school

> A comprehensive view of learning needs to include multiple factors: curricular and pedagogical approaches, strategies, programs, and policies, and also less tangible factors such as ideologies, attitudes and behaviors of teachers and students. All of these factors can promote or impede student learning.
>
> (Nieto, 1999)

As Sonia Nieto describes above, in any study of classroom learning several facets of the school environment should be addressed. The purpose of this is to better understand the larger context of the classroom experience, drawing on that knowledge to gain insight into the influences surrounding the students. All the descriptive information about the school and the district that we present in this chapter was true during the time this study was conducted.

School context

Mayfair Middle School (as mentioned earlier, all names of districts, schools, and students are fictitious), where this study was conducted, is part of the Foothill School District in the San Francisco Bay Area in California. The Foothill School District includes five towns with an approximate average enrollment during the four years of this study of 31,600 students. As of 1993, the Foothill district had a diverse student population with a racial and ethnic makeup of: 35.72% African American, 27.09% Caucasian, 18.62% Hispanic, 12.77% Asian and Pacific Islander, and 0.40% Native American (District records, March 1993). Mayfair is one of five junior high/middle schools in the district.

Mayfair is located in an area of the district populated mostly by middle-class, Caucasian families, but, at the time of this study, the school was primarily made up of African American students as a result of school restructuring which will be discussed. There are thirty-seven elementary schools and five senior high schools.

History of Mayfair Junior High

In 1986, Cleveland Junior High School, located in a lower-income neighborhood of the Foothill district, was closed due to a budget reduction. During the 1985–6 school year, Cleveland had an African American student population of 50%. Because of Cleveland's closure in 1986, the junior high school boundaries in the district were redefined. Those students living in the lower-income, downtown areas of the district were reassigned either to Mayfair Junior High School or to another junior high school nearer to their community (Personal communication with Foothill district administrator, 3/10/93). Also in 1986, Park Junior High School, located in the same mostly middle-class, Caucasian community as Mayfair, closed and remained closed for two years. That year, Park had an African American student population of 61%. Because it closed, many of the students who had attended Park were redirected to Mayfair. Between 1985 and 1989, the African American student population at Mayfair increased from 49% to 68%.

In addition, in 1987, a new superintendent took office in the Foothill district, and he initiated a district-wide program called the "System for Choice." One development under that system was the designation of a series of magnet schools throughout the district. As a part of the "System for Choice," Park Junior High School, near Mayfair, reopened in 1988 as a middle school with a highly publicized curriculum and school structure. As part of its "magnet school" designation, Park was required to have a student population whose percentages reflected the district as a whole, and the student population attending Park was determined on a first-come, first-served basis. Comparing the year it closed and the year it reopened, the student population at Park changed dramatically. As of October, 1989, 34% of the students at Park were African American while 42% were Caucasian compared to 68% African American and 12% Caucasian at Mayfair that same year. In 1992, 35% of the students at Park were African American and 31% were Caucasian compared to Mayfair which had 62% African American and 11% Caucasian.

There are several possible explanations for the large percentage of African American students at Mayfair compared to the Caucasian student population. Some of the Caucasian families living in the Mayfair area moved their children to Park Junior High School when it reopened in 1988. Other Caucasian families in the hills may have moved out of the area or they may have put their children in private schools. This shift in the previous Caucasian student population at Mayfair made it possible for the larger numbers of African American students from low-income, downtown communities to attend Mayfair.

Many of the African American students and other students from various minority groups, who live in the lower-income, downtown areas of this district and attend Mayfair, come to and from school on public transportation: on buses or on the rail system called Bay Area Rapid Transit (BART). The enrollment at Mayfair averaged 730 students until it became a middle school during the 1991–2 school year, when a small group of sixth grade students was added. The student population at the beginning of the 1992–3 school year was 949 students.

School structure

Under the district's "System for Choice" plan (1987–91), Mayfair was designated a University Laboratory School, a designation it kept despite the demise of the "System for Choice" plan in 1991. The University Laboratory program at Mayfair incorporated a number of elements from recent research on effective schools. It organized students into a core of classes called colleges where they worked on both academic and social skills. Typically, students took one chosen elective and a physical education class outside their college.

Each college was limited to 100–125 students. The students were placed in classes according to their "ranking" which was based on test scores and grades from upper elementary school. Each student was given a number between one and four with four being the strongest ranking and one the weakest. The counselors tried to group the students in their classes so that the fours and twos were together and the threes and ones were together. This grouping of students, then, was neither completely heterogeneous nor homogeneous.

The district administrators opposed homogeneous grouping, and the teachers at Mayfair adamantly opposed completely heterogeneous grouping after trying it for one year. This grouping of students at Mayfair, then, was a kind of compromise. There was a team of instructors for each college made up of a science, an English, a math, and a history teacher. The goal was for this team of teachers to work together to integrate the educational and social experiences of the students.

Student conflict at Mayfair

In terms of student conflict in the Mayfair school community, in the 1991–2 school year, gang activity was almost non-existent according to the principal (Personal communication, 11/17/92). There were individual student conflicts, but the students did not band together. As for vandalism, the most obvious example was graffiti found on the walls. Compared to the other junior high/middle schools in the district, Mayfair had only an average number of such incidents. According to the principal, during the 1991–2 school year, there were an unusually high number of fights on campus, however. These sometimes included quite vicious assaults without any apparent provocation. With the younger, sixth grade students attending Mayfair and no eighth grade students from the 1991–2 school year held back, the number of conflicts decreased the following year.

Student support systems

A number of programs, within the school and from outside, were available to support students who were having problems at Mayfair. There was a program provided by personnel within Mayfair entitled, "Suspension Alternative Class" (SAC). It was considered to be an option to suspension from school for students with consistent behavior problems. The students who chose SAC attended a self-contained, all-day class, taught by a full-time teacher hired specifically as the SAC teacher. When the students were in SAC, their regular teachers could provide them with make-up or current work, with which the designated teacher helped them if needed. If the students had nothing else to work on, the SAC teacher provided them with various English or math assignments.

In addition to the SAC program within Mayfair, there were services coming from outside of the school. A therapist from the YMCA and the district's mental health division was available two times a week, and there was a therapist available twice a week from "Gateway," an organization linking the mental health division and the Foothill district schools. There was also an intern counseling therapist from a nearby university who was on campus four days each week. These therapists provided counseling and support for students who had special problems with drug/substance abuse, dysfunctional families, etc.

Family involvement

In terms of family involvement in the decision-making and problem-solving needs at Mayfair, there were four key groups. One was the traditional Parent–Teacher Association (PTA). Its meetings on Saturdays, once a month, usually drew nineteen to twenty-one family members.

A second group was the School Advisory Council which met monthly in an advisory capacity for the "Chapter 1 program." To qualify for participation in the Chapter 1 program, students had to be members of a minority group and score below the fiftieth percentile in language, arts and/or math on the California Achievement Test (CAT). Typically, according to the principal, an average of seven family members attended those meetings on a regular basis. At the meetings, Mayfair staff and family members discussed the program and made programmatic and annual budgetary recommendations. The school plan was also approved by this council.

A third group was the site council, whose members made decisions about discretionary funds available to Mayfair. For example, they purchased books for the library and provided lunch for the faculty and staff on special occasions.

The fourth and last group participated on a magnet steering committee which was a Limited English Proficiency (LEP) advisory committee. This group met monthly to discuss recommendations for LEP programs. The budget was discussed and approved annually. This program was evaluated every year through the revisions of the school plan. Attendees included

Mayfair staff and family members. When combined, all these groups involved a very small number of family members from the school community – perhaps, in part, due to physical distance from the area where most resided.

School–university connections

In order to increase the school's effectiveness, it was the goal of Mayfair's University Laboratory program to forge educational partnerships between itself and the vast resources of the university and college community. Mayfair had programs with two local universities. One of the progams was the "Academic Talent Development Program" in which selected students attended accelerated math and language classes on the campus during the summer. The other program was called the "Partnership Program" in which students of color were given encouragement and support during the academic year. The goal of this program was to steer as many "under-represented" students of color toward college as possible.

The program that Mayfair offered in conjunction with the other university was called the "College Readiness Program" (CRP). This program was designed to help students develop strong study skills. It included tutoring and coaching on the Mayfair campus for students who had promise – according to teacher recommendation – and who were also members of a minority group.

Teacher profile

The faculty at Mayfair was primarily Caucasian. In the 1990–1 school year, for example, the racial make-up of the teachers was: 74% Caucasian, 25% African American, 2% Hispanic, and 0% Asian. In terms of gender breakdown, there were 63% women and 37% men that same year. The average age of the members of the faculty was 41. In terms of teaching experience, the average service in the district of the faculty that year was eight years and the average total years of teaching experience was eleven years (District records, 1990–1).

In the 1992–3 school year, the racial make-up at Mayfair had changed. There were more Caucasian and fewer African American teachers. During that year the faculty members were 44%

Caucasian women, 36% Caucasian men, 8.4% African American women, 6.7% African American men, and 5.0% Asian women (Personal communication with the principal of Mayfair, 4/22/93).

The teacher population at Mayfair was quite unstable. Mayfair actually reflected the high turnover rate across the district as a whole. Out of a total of 1,500 teachers, approximately 200 were new each year (Personal Communication with a district administrator, 3/10/93). At the beginning of the 1991–2 school year, out of fifty-seven teachers at Mayfair, 60 percent of them were new. There were a number of reasons for this teacher turnover. Because it had a reputation as a school with "a high minority population, many of whom were behavior problems," teachers considered Mayfair to be one of the "least desirable" schools in the district. Consequently, experienced teachers chose "more desirable" schools, and beginning teachers, lacking seniority, were often placed at Mayfair.

Also, on occasion, the district administrators decided at the end of the year to address budgetary constraints by laying off some of the teachers with the least amount of tenure. Sometimes, the newer staff at Mayfair were replaced by other teachers in the district who were involuntarily transferred to Mayfair. Another reason for turnover at Mayfair was because relatively new teachers sometimes decided to leave teaching for other careers.

In addition to the high teacher turnover at Mayfair, over the four-year period from 1987 to 1991, Mayfair had five principals. The fifth principal came to Mayfair during the 1991–2 school year and was the principal at Mayfair during the 1992–3 school year as well.

The instability of the teacher population and of the administrators at Mayfair made it difficult for consistent policies and programs to be established and continued over the years. Each change caused a certain amount of disruption along with anxiety and sometimes confusion on the part of the faculty and staff who stayed at Mayfair, and on the part of those who were new. Effective schools studies have demonstrated that this kind of anxiety and uncertainty caused by frequent turnover of teachers and administrators at a school comes through in the classroom and negatively affects student motivation and achievement (Edmonds, 1978).

Student profile

At the time of this study, the student population at Mayfair was predominantly African American from the inner city with a variety of other racial and ethnic groups represented. For example, the ethnic make-up in 1993 was: 63% African American, 13% Asian and Pacific Islander, 13% Caucasian, 8% Hispanic, 1% American Indian and Alaska Native, and 0.84% Filipino. The student grade point average at Mayfair typically fell at the midpoint in the district's cumulative junior high/middle school averages. To the principal's knowledge, over the years, no students actually dropped out of Mayfair when they were still living in the area. Of course, some students left Mayfair because they moved to a new location for one reason or another.

During all four years of this study, as Karen had requested, a large percentage of her students were considered "at-risk" of school failure based on their performance in upper elementary school. All of the African American students came from low-income communities in the inner city. Approximately 23 percent of the Mayfair families during the 1991–2 school year received Aid for Families with Dependent Children (AFDC).

During the first year of the project, in the 1990–1 school year, Karen had twenty-three seventh grade World History students. Eighteen students (approximately 75 percent) were African Americans, two were Asian, two were Caucasian, and one was Hispanic. There were ten girls and thirteen boys in the class. Five of the African American students were certified "gifted" (based on test scores) but were considered to be "low achievers" because of their performance record in elementary school. Thirty percent of the students in this cohort lived with a single parent or with a relative other than a parent.

The second (1991–2) cohort of students consisted of twenty-four African Americans, three Asians, and two Hispanics. There were no Caucasian students the second year. Karen had sixteen boys and thirteen girls that year – 29 students in all. A much higher percentage – 70 percent of the students in this cohort – lived with a single parent or with a relative other than a parent.

During the first year of this study, the students came to their World History class for 43 minutes of instruction every day for 180 days. During the second year, the class periods were extended to 55 minutes, since the school had to eliminate one period of electives due to budget constraints. In terms of the seventh grade history curriculum, the state framework mandated that the students be exposed to the heritages of several minorities, along with some European and Middle Eastern cultures – all during the Middle Ages except for Ancient Rome. Cultures included: Ancient Rome, the African empires of Ghana, Mali, and Songhai, Japan, China, India, and the American civilizations of the Aztecs, Mayans, and Incas.

In the third and fourth years of our study, Karen had one group of students whom she taught the third year in a seventh grade World History class and about half of the same group in the fourth year in an eighth grade US History class. Over the course of both years, most of the students who started with Karen at the beginning of the year remained in the class the entire year. However, there were a few students who moved away and others who moved into the Mayfair school boundaries in the middle of the year and over the summer after that third year. During both years this student turn-over caused the "class personality" to change temporarily.

In the third year, there were a total of thirty students: nineteen African American (63%), five Caucasian (17%), three Asian (10%), and three Hispanic (10%). There were fifteen boys and fifteen girls. In the fourth year, there were a total of twenty-one students: thirteen African American (62%), three Asian (14%), three Caucasian (14%), and two Hispanic (10%). There were fourteen boys and seven girls.

Overall, during this longitudinal portion of our study (the third and fourth years), there were fourteen students who were in Karen's class both years. Ten of those students became our "target students" who we interviewed on a regular basis. Like the group of students in the first two years of our study, all of the African American students came from the inner city, and many of them were considered "at risk" for school failure based on their grades in upper elementary school and on their test scores in fifth grade.

Chapter 5

Teacher action research

When Karen returned to teaching, she and Andrea designed a systematic teacher research process for collecting and analyzing data about our students. We wanted to document accurately the implementation of our alternative teaching strategies. We describe our procedure in the section below.

Data collection

In our study, three accounts of the classroom experience were used because we wanted to represent the voices of all of those involved. Specifically, data were collected each year from Karen in the form of a reflective journal, from an assisting observer in the form of classroom observation notes, and from the students in interviews and questionnaires. Narrative inquiry, which seeks the personal perspective of each participant in a study, was the primary method of data collection (Connelly and Clandinin, 1990). Multiple accounts provide an especially rich view of classroom experiences. Using three perspectives (teacher, assisting observer, and students) also triangulates the data which increases the validity of the findings (Miles and Huberman, 1984).

Sources of data

Teacher journal

The teacher-produced data for this study came from the journal entries Karen wrote, including observations and analyses. At the end of each teaching day, Karen wrote down aspects of the classroom experience which included the content covered and any responses by the African American students that might be attributable to any of the four alternative teaching strategies. After summarizing her recollections of what had happened each day in her interactions with her students inside or outside of class, Karen wrote a reflective analysis. She focused on daily summarized experiences, considering the reasons why she and the students responded in certain ways and also noted any new questions she had as a result of that day's experiences. In addition, in the third and fourth years, Karen commented on any observed obstacles to student motivation. Here is an example of her journal notes, written the fourth year, on Tuesday, February 13 1996:

AGENDA

1   *Receive small book,* To Be A Slave

2   *Brainstorm "Impressions of Slavery"*

3   *Share ideas*

4   *Look at pictures in book: pp. 19, 23, 34, 41, 47, 67 and add to list of impressions (these pages have pictures of slaves under a variety of circumstances)*

5   *Roots, part 2, for 10 minutes*

6   *Read in book, pp. 16–18*

COMMENTS

Many of the students seem intrigued with the book. I gave them about 3 minutes to write down any thoughts they had at this point about what slavery must have been like – anywhere in the world at any time in history. I had passed out lined paper to those who needed it. The ideas the students came up with really seemed like they came from the heart.

Next, I had them look at certain pages in the little book which had pictures of slaves in America. I asked them to add to their list if new thoughts came to their minds. After about 5 minutes we discussed what they came up with. The participation during all of this came from mostly African American students except for one White student.

At this point, I showed about 10 minutes of Roots, *part 2, when Kunta Kinte has arrived off the slave ship in America and is sold on the auction block. After that part of the story, I asked them to share any additional ideas they thought of. They had pretty much exhausted their ideas after looking at the pictures, but there were a few added.*

The last activity was reading the prologue to the book. It was very sobering about how cruel slavery was and about how the story of African American history is so seldom told.

HIGHLIGHTS

How serious the class was about the slavery experience and how open some of the students were with their feelings about it. I sensed that those who spoke up really felt a connection with their past and with the suffering that their ancestors had to go through. It was intense in the class but not tense. I've never seen the kids more focused or engaged. I think that's because this topic feels really relevant and important to them and they are almost hungry for it. The Caucasian, Asian, and Hispanic kids didn't seem uncomfortable at all. It didn't seem like the African American kids were angry – just keenly interested.

OTHER THOUGHTS

It is so exciting for me as a teacher when my students are as engaged and intense as they were today. This is what good teaching is all about. It's just so unusual that I am able to present the subject matter in a way that grabs the students. I have so much to learn about that (after 26 years??!!).

Assisting observers' notes

While Karen kept her daily journal over the four years of our study, observers visited the class, stayed the entire period, and took comprehensive notes. During the first two years of the study, one of the collaborating researchers from the university (Andrea came the first year) visited the classroom twice each week. In the third and fourth years, a fellow seventh grade World History teacher (whose classroom Karen was sharing), was present in the class every day as part of Karen's Spencer Postdoctoral Fellowship. The assisting researchers observed the classroom interactions and wrote a description and analysis of those experiences, including any responses by the African American students to the alternative strategies introduced by Karen. Here is an example of the assisting observer's notes on the same day, February 13 1996, as Karen described in her journal earlier:

OBSERVATION COMMENTS

Absent: Richard (SAC), Tardy: Michelle, Mike, and Gerald

(1) Bell. Karen says that Michelle, a classroom officer, is absent and asks if someone would volunteer to pass out the folders. Peter volunteers to pass out the folders. Flag salute and announcements. Michelle comes in at 8:34. Karen has her pass out paper. Karen says to the class, "OK, on your piece of lined paper, I'm going to have you brainstorm about slavery. Any time and anywhere in the world. This week we discuss slavery in particular in the United States." Karen puts on the overhead a transparency and writes: "Impressions of Slavery – List #1." Michelle yells out, "Mrs. Teel, I don't understand!" Karen says to her, "When you think of slavery, put down the words that you think of." Michelle says, "Prejudice." Karen says, "OK." Michelle asks, "Can I put ugly?" Karen tells her to put anything that she wants. Michelle says, "Don't get mad when I write down." Karen had set the timer for 5 minutes for them to brainstorm on their papers. The timer goes off. Karen tells them, "OK, whatever came to your mind. First round."

(2) Karen lists the words the students have put down for the brainstorm. Gerald comes in at 8:45.

- bondage and chains
- laziness (slave owner)
- ugly and prejudice (white people; slave owners)
- plantations

- hard labor
- unfree, fear
- no pay
- weariness, pain
- sickness, whips

Karen takes a minute to tell Gerald to get a piece of paper and write down his impressions of slavery.

- ignorance, short patience
- master

(3) Karen says, "OK, so now that you have thought about your impressions of slavery, before the video, look at pictures in *To Be A Slave*. See if there is anything else that you want to add to this list." Karen gives them time to look at the pictures in the book. Mike comes in at 8:50.

(4) Karen has the students add to the list:

- abusive, naked, for sale
- cruelty, separation
- unfairly treated, work early age
- KKK (Killing black folks)
- hot and sweaty
- burnt crosses (KKK)

Karen says that at this point they are going to watch *Roots*, part 2 and see if it adds to their impressions of slavery.

(5) Karen reviews that *Roots*, part 1 was about African village life and that most of the slaves came from West Africa. Mike and Michelle are talking and Karen reminds them that they can talk the last 5 minutes of the class. So Karen brings them up to the part in the video when Kunta Kinte is being sold in Maryland. Karen tells them to add to their list if they see anything else. The class watches *Roots*, part 2 for about 5 minutes. Karen tells them, "OK, so tomorrow you'll keep watching this; that was to give you a visual of what it was like." Jasmine says, "It's not time to go." Karen says that they are going to read in the book.

(6) Karen tells the class, "Keep in mind these African people were in an advanced civilization. *Roots* is based on Alex Haley's ancestors." Karen tells them to open the book to the title page. Michelle says, "Can I read first?" Karen tells her, "Jasmine asked first. There is a quote I want to read on the next page about ancestry." Karen reads the quote. Jasmine reads the section about African trade. Michelle reads the next section. Karen explains to the class how Native Americans wouldn't cooperate when the colonists tried to get them to work on their farms. Paul says that it is the last 5 minutes. Karen says that there is 1 minute left.

REFLECTIONS

1   I thought that this brainstorming is a good way to let the students get all of the negative feelings expressed without being concerned about what the teacher (White) might think; there is no wrong answer; just their own impression. I think Karen has made the students feel comfortable enough to be honest with their feelings.

2   I was impressed with the type of words that the students were using to describe their impressions. Here again I'm impressed with Michelle's willingness to participate. Paul seemed to get a little bit more engaged in this activity. I think he had some interest in this area.

3   I liked using *Roots*, part 2 for the visual experience; it is one thing to talk about the cruelty and inhumane treatment of slaves. It is much harder to watch the reality of the slave auction.

In comparing these two descriptions of the classroom experiences and reflections on them written by Karen and the assisting observer on February 13 1996, differences and similarities in their write-ups are clear. Since Karen had to wait until after class to write down her observations, she tended to give a general description of the activities that took place during class. On the other hand, the assisting observer, who wrote down her observations during class time, gave a more detailed description of individual student responses and individual events. In terms of similarities, however, when they reflected on the overall classroom experience, each of them offered general, personal impressions.

Student interviews

In addition to the journal and observation data, during all four years of this study, data were collected in individual and small group interviews. The interview questions during all four years pertained to the four alternative teaching strategies Karen was using and how the students who had become "high achievers" were interpreting their improved grades. During the third and fourth years, questions were also asked about possible obstacles that might be interfering with the motivation and high achievement of the "lower-achieving" students. The interview questions focusing on the teaching strategies were about student opportunities to improve their work, teacher emphasis on effort, choice of assignments, multiple ways for students to demonstrate their knowledge, and student explanations for their higher grades.

Interview questions regarding possible obstacles to student motivation and achievement dealt mostly with peer disapproval of high grades. Questions were also asked about what the students' and their parents' or guardians' grade aspirations were compared to the lowest grade they would still find acceptable.

The assisting observer conducted informal individual interviews about the classroom experience with ten of the African American students selected randomly for each of the first three years. During the fourth year, most of the targeted students from the third year were still in Karen's class. The assisting observer also conducted group interviews each year with four groups of five students each. The groups represented different levels of classroom achievement based on grades and test scores from upper elementary school. Each interview lasted approximately 15 minutes. All these interviews were audio-taped, summarized, and later transcribed. (See Appendix A for an example of an interview protocol.)

Student questionnaires

Along with the teacher's journal, assisting observers' notes, and interview data, at regular intervals during all four years, questionnaire data were collected from the students. During the first two years, these questionnaires consisted primarily of open-ended questions related to the four alternative teaching strategies. During the third and fourth years, as in the individual and group interviews, the questions focused on two factors that might prevent stronger student academic self-confidence. The two factors were: (1) our students' belief that they received good grades due to easy work rather than their ability (Weiner, 1977), and (2) the large number of high grades in the class which might lessen their value. These questions also focused on potential obstacles to high achievement in the class.

Four different questionnaires, collaboratively designed by Karen, Andrea, and Dr. Covington, were given to all of the students at the end of each quarter. The students were asked questions such as how they liked the grading system, how they liked choices in their assignments, and how they liked reading literature written by and about people from their own cultural background. In the third and fourth years, they were also asked questions about peer pressure and their grade aspirations. The questionnaire responses were tallied each time and the results of each one were compared to and coordinated with the other sources of data. (See Appendix B for a sample student questionnaire.)

Multiple narratives, multiple views: some dilemmas

As a teacher researcher, Karen believed that it was important to assess the impact of our innovative classroom approach through collaborative data collection and analysis in order to strengthen the legitimacy of the study. Dilemmas can arise, however, whenever the different classroom researchers (teacher, assisting observers, and students) have conflicting ways of looking at and describing the classroom experiences. For example, as we pointed out earlier in comparing Karen's notes with those of the assisting observer, the teacher may focus on the class as a whole in assessing the students' responses to the curriculum, whereas the assisting researchers may be interested in the behavior of individual students. Also, the students may question the legitimacy of innovative teaching strategies (even if they are receiving better grades) because other previous and current teachers have not used them, and because they do not see themselves as successful students. This was a dilemma that we struggled with in our attempt to present a composite view of the classroom experiences over the course of this study.

Another problem arose with assessing the impact of Karen's classroom approach on her students. By comparing her observations, impressions, and conclusions with those of the assisting observers during the first two years of the study, it was clear that because Karen was in the classroom with the students daily, she inevitably saw many things they did not see. Assisting researchers typically visit classes sporadically, perhaps on a regular weekly basis but sometimes less often. Since classroom experiences are often different from one day to the next, one could question whether or not a "part-time" visitor to the class can get an accurate picture of the dynamics of the class. Hence, the legitimacy of "outsiders' " conclusions has sometimes been questioned by classroom teachers. It was in an attempt to combat this problem that Karen asked a fellow teacher at her school to be a *daily* assisting observer in her classroom during the third and fourth years of the study. This was highly unusual.

The students also participated in the data collection process. As recipients of the strategies we had designed, they were in a unique position to offer an alternative perspective regarding the merits of our approach and the obstacles that prevented them from succeeding. This is another reason why the students are an invaluable source of data through the questionnaires they fill out and through interviews with them. Obviously, except for the days when they are absent, like the teacher, they are regular observers in their own classrooms.

Along with the problems described above of the limited perspective of assisting observers who visit the classroom on a weekly basis, there are also limitations to the perspectives of teachers and students. Because they become an integral part of classroom experiences, teachers and their students may well find it hard to separate themselves from the overall picture in order to notice nuances – variations in attitudes and behavior – which inevitably exist in a classroom with an average attendance of anywhere from twenty to thirty-five students.

At the same time as teachers become an integral part of the classroom experience, as teacher researchers they have an additional challenge: they also must adopt a kind of "double vision." This is because they are taking on a dual role in the classroom simultaneously: the role of teacher and of researcher. As teachers, they implement the lesson plans they have designed, and, if they don't go well, they have the responsibility for improving them. As researchers, they try to assess, analyze, and theoretically explain the students' responses to the lessons. Based on her experiences with this dual role, Magdalene Lampert (1991: 9) describes some possible dilemmas:

> So far, I have been talking about how being a teacher affects how I teach. Writing in a voice that allows me to move back and forth between two sets of values and two sets of norms for how one talks about phenomena involves me as a teacher in seeing the events that occur in my classroom in two ways. I bring the curiosity of the research community together with the responsibility of the teaching community, and sometimes these values clash – not only in what I write, but in my thinking about what to do.

Here is an excerpt from Karen's own notes during the beginning of the second year of this study when she was experiencing the dilemma of her "dual role":

> *Just as an aside, I am feeling more and more schizophrenic these days about my dual role of teacher and researcher. It's funny how smart, intellectual, theoretical, and confident I feel as a researcher and yet how demoralized, beaten down, "clueless," and lost I sometimes feel as a teacher. The worlds are so very different. We can think whatever we want and feel comfortable with those views. However, dealing with 20–35 teenagers, attempting to address all of the concerns we have about them and the potential we know they have is incredibly challenging and quite frustrating. Maybe the biggest part of the problem is that I don't completely understand yet what is going on. I don't understand why some days last week were miserable while others were a joy. How can the same students act so mature, motivated, and engaged one day and then act like little kids bent on sabatoging a lesson on another day??*
>
> (Karen's Journal, 10/91)

All these questions and concerns about accurately portraying the classroom experiences through multiple perspectives had to be taken into account in the data analysis procedures. These procedures were the key to providing as objective a portrayal as possible of classroom life during the four years of our study.

Discrepancies in each of our accounts of these classroom experiences had to be reconciled in some way. Because of the complexity of this task, we decided to concentrate on the impressions we all had in common, believing that those impressions would be the most accurate assessment of the experiences. Below, we explain the procedures we used to analyze our data.

Data analysis

From each source of data, during all four years of the study, we were looking for repeated positive student responses relating to the four alternative teaching strategies: non-competitive classroom structure with effort-based grading, multiple performance opportunities, increased student responsibility and choice, and validation of cultural heritage. During the third and fourth years, we were also looking for the obstacles already mentioned. The participants purposely decided to only code for the clearly positive student responses to our strategies even though the teacher and students experienced various problems over the course of the year. We wanted to identify and report successful strategies so that other educators might use them as well.

A strategy was considered successful when a majority of the students in the class as a whole were observed to be enthusiastic, engaged, and learning, and when such positive responses were also indicated in student interviews and on student questionnaires. When there was a majority of negative responses to the strategy (apathy, disruption, complaints) it was considered unsuccessful. Our system of data analysis is explained below.

Coding system

For this study, we used a coding system to analyze the data from all four sources: Karen's journal, assisting observer notes, student interviews, and student questionnaires. We designed our coding system to address each of the four alternative teaching strategies: (1) a non-competitive classroom structure with effort-based grading, (2) multiple performance opportunities, (3) increased responsibility and choice, and (4) validation of cultural heritage. We used distinct criteria to determine positive student responses to these four strategies. These criteria, listed below, were specifically related to student motivation.

*Strategy 1: non-competitive classroom structure with
effort-based grading – criteria*

- Frequency and quality of participation in classroom discussions
- Level of effort on individual assignments
- Effect of improved grades on sense of academic potential
- Response to positive feedback and fair treatment from teacher

Strategy 2: multiple performance opportunities – criteria

- Degree of interest in the lesson
- Willingness to reveal previously unrecognized talents and strengths

*Strategy 3: increased student responsibility and choice –
criteria*

- Willingness to assist in the classroom
- Responses to choice

Strategy 4: validation of cultural heritage – criteria

- Time on task during sustained silent multicultural reading program
- Volunteering for book talks focused on self-selected culturally relevant materials
- Student engagement in discussions about culturally relevant issues

Procedure for analyzing specific data sources

Teacher journal/observer notes

Using the "constant comparative method" (Glaser and Strauss, 1967), we summarized on a daily basis the individual findings within the separate sets of notes taken by Karen and the assisting observer. We identified positive student responses to our teaching strategies. In the third and fourth years, we also identified comments about obstacles to increasing academic self-confidence by our "high achievers" and obstacles to "high achievement" by our "low achievers." According to the "constant comparative method," as data are collected over a designated period of time, the researcher determines tentative results. Then, as new data are collected, the researcher constantly compares those results with the earlier ones and adjusts the "current findings" accordingly.

For example, in our study, every month the two separate sets of notes were compared by each of us for similarities in findings. These similarities were listed each month, and, as any of them were repeatedly found during the course of the year, the number of months in which they were mentioned was noted. At the end of the school year, patterns of responses, noted during at least five different months, were considered to be evidence that the teaching strategies mentioned were having a positive impact, and, during the third and fourth years, that the identified obstacles should be taken seriously.

Student interviews/questionnaires

Using the previously listed criteria, the student interview transcriptions and student questionnaire data were also analyzed. Karen and Andrea listed the positive responses to the alternative teaching strategies that were mentioned by a majority of students and the obstacles mentioned. As explained earlier, student questionnaires consisted of open-ended questions, and the answers to these questions, as well as the interview responses provided us with additional qualitative data to analyze.

Triangulation of data sources

By collecting data from the teacher researcher, assisting observer, and students, we had three unique perspectives to examine. As mentioned previously, this method of collecting, aggregating, and analyzing the data is known as triangulation and is thought to increase the validity of the findings (Miles and Huberman, 1984).

After the journal and observation data had been analyzed, Karen and Andrea compared those findings to the student interview and questionnaire data analyses. This was done by comparing the repeated positive student responses and obstacles identified in both sets of data. Finally, at the end of each school year, we put together a composite list of those positive responses and obstacles (at the end of the third and fourth years) that had been mentioned repeatedly over the course of the year by Karen and the assisting observer and that were corroborated by the students in interviews and in questionnaires.

Discussion

During all four years of our study, our different cohorts of students responded positively to particular aspects of our alternative teaching approach. In many cases, motivation increased as did the quality of student performance and apparent academic self-confidence. Those positive findings will be reported in the next chapter.

Chapter 6

Realizing student potential with alternative strategies

> Again, when these students are given the opportunity to brain-storm together, they come up with much fascinating and right on target information. If they feel safe, and know that they won't be criticized for what they say, but rather supported and valued, they are unafraid to express their wealth of knowledge. They do this quite eloquently.
>
> (Andrea's Notes, 5/6/91)

This chapter will discuss the positive responses – particularly during the first two years of the study – that many students had to the alternative teaching strategies used in Karen's classroom. Each teaching strategy will be examined separately with conclusions reached based on the criteria outlined in Chapter 5 and shown in Table 6.1 (p. 50).

Student comments in class, on surveys and in interviews as well as entries from Karen's journal and the observers' notes will be used to provide evidence of the effectiveness of each teaching strategy. We believe strongly that students can directly provide us with many of the answers we are looking for if we just give them the opportunity to express themselves, *and we listen.*

Table 6.1 Criteria for the new teaching strategies

Strategy		Criteria	
1	Non-competitive classroom with effort-based grading	1	Frequency and quality of participation
		2	Level of effort on assignments
		3	Effect of improved grades on sense of academic potential
		4	Response to positive feedback and fair treatment from the teacher
2	Multiple performance opportunities	1	Degree of interest in the lesson
		2	Willingness to reveal previously unrecognized talents and strengths
3	Increased student responsibility and choice	1	Willingness to assist in the class
		2	Response to choice
4	Validation of cultural heritage	1	Time on task during multicultural reading program
		2	Volunteering for book talks
		3	Engagement in discussions about culturally relevant issues

Student responses to the alternative strategies

Strategy 1: Non-competitive classroom structure with effort-based grading

Criterion 1: Frequency and quality of participation in classroom discussions

Frequency and quality of participation were noted by recording how many students participated in a given discussion and examples of particularly articulate and astute comments. Based on this data, we found that a growing number of students slowly became bolder and clearer in their opinions and were more tolerant of each other's ideas.

During individual and group interviews and on the questionnaire given at the end of each school year, a majority of the students indicated that they were participating more frequently in class discussions because of the expanded opportunities for discussion, because of the credit they received for participating, and because Karen was very respectful toward their comments. For example, here is how one student explained his comfort level "I feel more comfortable because we get to speak more because we have more chances to speak" (Student Questionnaire, 4/91). Another student replied on a questionnaire administered at the end of the second year: "Yes, because I'm used to speaking now." Other students mentioned that they preferred sharing their learning orally rather than in writing.

> I would talk because when I talk I can say everything, you know, cause when I write it down, I leave out stuff, but when I'm talking everything that pops up in my head comes out, and I can express myself better.
>
> (Student Interview, 5/30/91)

Our data also revealed that class brainstorming sessions on topics that interested the students were very productive – as indicated in Andrea's notes at the beginning of this chapter. Most students became highly engaged during these sessions, allowing themselves to explore ideas, questions, and issues freely. When topics appeared to be relevant in any way to their own lives, students seemed to grasp their meanings more easily and responded more enthusiastically. Karen noted at the beginning of the second year:

> *What a great time I had today! The students stayed with me the entire period, especially when we were imagining ourselves as archaeologists. They love to brainstorm and to have each and every one of their ideas validated. I had to stop each discussion so that we could move on to another aspect of the topic. I was very impressed with their enthusiasm, patience, and rich ideas.*
>
> (Karen's Journal, 9/10/91)

The more students practiced "thinking out loud," and the more they were praised and given credit for it, the more effort many made and the more willing they were to take risks in their sharing of ideas. As time went on, the level of discussions became more sophisticated. Not surprisingly, it appeared that the more students practiced expressing their ideas orally, the better they got at it.

In addition, a dynamic developed during these discussions in which students drew from each other's comments to expand on their own ideas as Andrea noted at the end of the first year:

> When the subject material presented is relevant to the lives of these kids, they respond dramatically. Discussions are multi-leveled, continuous, and provoke many, who normally do not speak out, to participate. There is actually an air of excitement in the room. These students enjoy sharing their opinions, and when they cooperate with each other, the knowledge base constructed together is amazing.
>
> (Andrea's Notes, 5/2/91)

Criterion 2: Level of effort on individual assignments

The emphasis placed on effort as a significant factor in their final grade seemed to encourage many students to try harder. We assessed level of effort on individual assignments by how hard students worked on each assignment, the length of time spent before students turned work in, and the quality of their homework. Based on our data, we found over the years that the majority of students became more persevering on class assignments as the school year progressed, including on tests. In addition, as the year advanced, more and more students were willing to revise their work for a higher grade.

On a questionnaire given to the students in January of the first year, 16 out of 18 students indicated that if they get a good grade it is because they tried very hard. In addition, all of those completing the questionnaire wrote that the more they try the more they learn. In explaining why he gets a better grade in this class than in most of his other classes, one student wrote: "I try harder in this class than other classes." On a questionnaire in April of the first year, one student explained why he feels smarter in this class:

> There's no word for it but the work we do in this class you grade us like; If the first answer for a question is right its +3. If you got the second a little right it +2 or +1. Other classes its wrong.
>
> (Student Questionnaire, 4/30/91)

On a questionnaire given in May of the second year, 17 out of 25 students answered that anyone could get an "A" in this class if they worked hard enough. Ten of those 17 explained that if you work hard in this class, you'll get a good grade. One student wrote, "everybody can work up to the ability." On that same questionnaire, 21 out of 25 indicated that they had been able to improve their grade by re-doing work. Clearly, the students saw the benefits of effort. It appeared that our intervention changed the predominant pattern of "low-achieving" students who typically attribute success to luck or task ease and not to effort (Friend and Neale, 1972; Weiner, 1972, 1977).

Over the course of the year, student effort did increase which led to more "time on task" and engagement. Two male students, during the second year, started out the year with negative motivation. They rarely completed assignments and were often disruptive during class time. Toward the end of the year, they became exemplary students:

> *One aside: Maurice and Ralph have turned into such great students! They are both working hard and turning in most assignments.*
>
> (Karen's Journal, 5/27/92)

Criterion 3: Effect of improved grades on sense of academic potential

Most students received higher grades in this class than they had in upper elementary school and in their other seventh grade classes. Also, their grades in this class improved over the course of the year. In questionnaires and interviews, the majority of students said they wanted to receive an "A" or "B." When they actually saw those grades on assignments, progress reports, and on report cards they expressed excitement and pride. Hence, one of the recurring themes throughout our data was that good grades excite and please most students. This theme is shown here in Andrea's notes the first year:

> It seemed to me that the class as a whole was happy with their grades. I got the feeling that most of them hadn't done so well in previous classes. One student was dancing around with joy.
>
> (Andrea's Notes, 11/5/90)

At first, even "C's" were well-received by students who were getting "D's" and "F's" in their other classes. However, most students received increasingly higher grades during the year because effort was emphasized. Students were allowed to re-do work and to turn work in late with a minor penalty. The excitement and pride in higher grades led to a greater willingness by these students to try hard on future assignments (Student Interviews, Years One and Two). As each year progressed, students began to express disappointment in grades which used to be acceptable (such as "C's"). The norm in the class became good grades as indicated by the assisting observer during the second year:

> Grades were a hot topic for the kids today. They had received them during break. Ralph had a strong reaction to receiving a "C", which to him was like an "F". It is interesting how the meaning of a grade shifts given the class. In most other classes I am sure that a "C" is okay. However, in this class, where the perception is that everyone gets "A's" and "B's", a "C" is a bad grade.
>
> (Observer's Notes, 4/20/92)

This development in students' responses to "C's" is evidence of a change in their perception of their potential to succeed. Based on teacher journal and assisting observer data, when they received disappointing grades in this class as the year progressed, most students did not give up as easily as they did earlier in the year. Judging by comments that many students made during individual and group interviews during the study, it also appeared that receiving a good grade in this class motivated many of the students to work harder in their other classes:

> I already [raised my grade] in this class. A "B" is good enough. But now in the other classes ... I need to work much harder than what I am now.
>
> (Small Group Student Interview, 5/27/92)

In interviews, the majority of students attributed their success partly to the encouragement they received to re-do work completed below the standards expected by the teacher, and to turn in late work with only a moderate penalty. When asked on a questionnaire if he was getting a better grade in this class, a student answered "yes," and explained his higher grade like "I am more motivated because you give me higher grades than other teachers."

On a questionnaire completed in February of the second year, the students were asked whether they thought the teacher considered them to be smart and how they knew. The majority of students marked yes. Here are some examples of their explanations: "Yes, because I made a 'B' in this classroom and didn't make no 'F'"; "Yes, because I get 'A's and 'B's"; "Because if I wasn't I wouldn't get the kind of grades I get in this class." "In other classes they grade weird and I understand you more than other teachers"; "Because I didn't think I was very good but when I got an 'A' I felt good."

On that same questionnaire, half of the students attributed their good grades to their ideas. The question was: "Do you think you have good ideas in this class?" One student marked "yes," and here is how she explained her answer: "Because I made a 'B' in here for ideas and work." These comments indicate the connection most students made between their grades and academic self-worth.

Criterion 4: Response to positive feedback and fair treatment from teacher

During all four years of this study, based on Karen's journal entries, the assisting observer's notes, and on student interview and questionnaire data, we came to the conclusion that all our students appreciated Karen's efforts to encourage them to do their best and the way she always tried to treat everyone equally and fairly. Here are some examples of student feedback around these issues.

During an interview at the end of the first year, one student said that [the teacher] is "always ready to praise them and reward them, and this creates a positive environment." In interviews conducted at the end of the second year, when asked what their teacher was like, students made these comments: "[She] is fair and treats everyone equally." "She takes time to help students, cares about students, and calls their parents." On one questionnaire completed during the middle of the second year, the students were asked whether or not they believe that the teacher thinks they are smart and how they can tell. Here are some of their responses. "She tells me almost every day"; "Because she believes in us. And she makes us feel like we are smart and she treat us with respect and everyone wants respect"; "I think she understands the way we think"; "Well I try to be as smart as I can in all my classes but this one is just better." Student comments were similar to the ones above in the last two years of the study as well.

Strategy 2: Multiple performance opportunities

Criterion 1: Degree of interest in the lesson

On occasion, when it seemed necessary in order to provide content in as efficient a manner as possible, Karen used traditional pedagogy, such as a lecture. According to Karen's journal and assisting observer data, when that type of traditional teaching method was used in the World History class, the majority of African American students' degree of interest was consistently lower. This further confirmed our findings about multiple performance opportunities. Many often did not participate, did not try, and were more uncooperative. On the other hand, when Karen used more innovative approaches to the subject matter (such as simulation games, skits, creative projects, and book talks), the majority of the students would consistently become more cooperative, more on-task, and more vocal. This excerpt from Karen's journal describes positive student response to multiple performance opportunities:

> The atmosphere in the class today along with the students' behavior and attitudes were quite a contrast with yesterday. The students really became engaged in the planning of their skits, and it seemed that each member of each group made their own unique contribution to the skit.
>
> (Karen's Journal, 5/14/91)

Many students clearly enjoyed demonstrating their oral, leadership, acting, and artistic skills. One of the students expressed the following in an interview:

> I like making up skits in a way because it's better than writing it. I can show it, and it is better showing it or saying it. When

you're writing sometimes you don't understand, but when you can express it out, then you can say well I understand. When other people express it out, then you can say well I understand what they mean because they showin' it instead of just writing it because they don't have the right words to say.

(Student Interview, 5/30/91)

In groups during the year, when participating in simulation games, most students appeared to be motivated, engaged, and learning. For example, during both years of this study, the students played the game "Starpower," a game in which the students end up in one of three groups based on accumulated power and wealth. During the first year of the study, once the students realized that one select group would rule over the rest, some of them delivered impassioned speeches about the rights of all members of society no matter how poor and seemingly powerless they might be. During the course of this activity (which went on for about one week), all of the students in both years were thoroughly engaged and motivated.

I think this kind of experience for the students is the key to motivation in schools. There was clear structure to the game and yet a great deal of freedom within the process for the students. They had to think and act on their own, to create their own position.

(Karen's Journal, 4/18/91)

Criterion 2: Willingness to reveal previously unrecognized talents and strengths

Based on observations of discussions, skits, book talks, and group activities – and on student interviews and questionnaires – the majority of students clearly recognized and thrived on the opportunities they had in this class to demonstrate their knowledge in a variety of ways. As one student said:

The best way for me to share something, you know, I just got to talk it out, you know some people draw, do other things, but I gotta talk to somebody, tell 'em.

(Student Interview, 5/29/91)

During the second year, the assisting observer commented on one of the student's special talents. At the time, this student was reading on the third grade reading level and was struggling with writing:

> I found that Jerry was superb at the map exercise and had little trouble with the instructions after a little help starting. I think that he would be good as a "map expert" – helping other students with problems with the map exercises. In this way, his ability could be recognized.
>
> (Observer's Notes, 5/15/92)

At another time during the second year, the teacher commented on the pleasure the students seemed to take in doing art projects. Many of them demonstrated their imaginative and artistic abilities in completing these projects. *"Students worked well for the most part today. They were really engaged in designing their own African masks"* (Karen's Journal, 3/19/92).

Strategy 3: Increased student responsibility and choice

Criterion 1: Willingness to assist in the classroom

Many students enthusiastically volunteered to be class officers during all four years of the study, and, over the course of the year, more and more students participated. During the two-week period when the students were class officers, they seemed to take their positions seriously and to enjoy the responsibility. Nearly all of them appeared to grow in confidence as a result of having these positions.

> *Based on a discussion with another teacher, I decided to ask the new president of the class to lead the reading and discussion activity. He agreed. He stood up at the podium, read the agenda, and then called on students to read. I was particularly pleased with the president's facility for leading the class. He seemed to relish the role, and was assertive and fair. I always feel so much more comfortable when the students are sharing the spotlight.*
>
> (Karen's Journal, 9/10/91)

These impressions by Karen and the assisting observer were corroborated by a majority of students in interviews and on questionnaires.

Criterion 2: Responses to choice

In the majority of cases, when the students were allowed to choose their own books, their own projects, or their own questions to answer, they took the work more seriously. In interviews and on questionnaires, most students made positive comments about these experiences. Here is one example:

> You probably can do something better if you draw a picture or a skit or talk about it. If you have a choice, then you really want to do it, and you can express yourself more in what you are trying to do.
>
> (Student Interview, 5/30/91)

Most students were more willing to cooperate under these circumstances because they felt they had some control over the situation (Thomas, 1980; Marshall and Weinstein, 1984). Here is an excerpt from the teacher's journal about the influence of choice on the students:

> *I am enjoying this class more and more, and I am very excited about the reading program. The students seem motivated to read when they can choose their own book and go at their own pace.*
>
> (Karen's Journal, 11/13/90)

Another example of this positive student response to choice was during March of the second year of the study. Karen wanted to do a project requiring the use of the newspaper every other Thursday. Each time the idea was presented to the students, many of them complained. Finally, Karen asked the students what they would like to do with the newspaper. The students brainstormed several options that Karen found acceptable, and then they voted. The next day, on Thursday, there were few complaints and most students worked as well as they had on any project all year.

Most students informed us that when they have choices they are willing to work harder. The assisting observer noted the following in a summary of an interview discussion around this topic with a small group of students: "They all agreed that students might be more motivated if they had more choices" (Observer's Notes, 6/1/92). In addition, according to interview and questionnaire data, it appeared that most students felt teachers who gave them choices showed more respect for them. Here is an excerpt from the assisting observer's notes commenting on an interview with a student in which this topic came up:

> Sonia strongly felt that the teacher does give students choices and that she does not have choices in her other classes. She said that the other teachers "do not care." It seemed that choice was associated with how much the teacher cares about the students. She mentioned a few assignments that involved lots of choice.
>
> (Observer's Notes, 6/8/92)

Strategy 4: Validation of cultural heritage

Criterion 1: Time on task during sustained silent multicultural reading program

Judging by the data, most students clearly enjoyed reading books about people from their same cultural backgrounds. Our experiences with these students corroborate the latest research on the importance for all students of cultural validation (Boateng, 1990; Delpit, 1995; Howe, 1992; Ladson-Billings, 1994; Ogbu, 1990). The African American students, in particular, almost invariably chose books about African Americans. Some selections were biographies about such figures as Harriet Tubman, George Washington Carver, Jackie Robinson, Bo Jackson, and Dr. Martin Luther King Jr. Other selections were examples of historical fiction dealing with African Americans such as *Escape to Freedom* (Ossie, 1978).

On a questionnaire in May, the first year, one African American student wrote: "I liked reading about slavery and about how people live back in the past." Based on interview and questionnaire data, having access to several choices of stories about people from their own cultural heritage and having the opportunity to read about them and talk about their contributions appears to have strengthened many students' sense of identity.

During an interview in the first year, one student described how discouraging he thinks it is to African American students when none of their books in school discuss their culture:

> 'cause they probably have like our people don't do nothing if they don't know nothing about theirselves. They probably say Black people can't do nothing anyway, so why should I try to do something?
>
> (Student Interview, 5/23/91)

On a questionnaire at the end of the second year, when asked how they feel about reading books about people from their own race, all the students indicated that they liked such an opportunity. For example, two African American students wrote: "I feel nice because most books are by White People." "It is nice to here something good about my race some time."

Criterion 2: Volunteering for book talks focused on self-selected culturally relevant materials

According to Karen's journal, the assisting observer's notes, and interview and questionnaire data, "book talks," presented weekly on a voluntary basis by the students, were one of the highlights of the classroom experience. Students gave rich, articulate descriptions of their books. African American students appeared to be very proud to tell about the success stories of certain African Americans including those about the courage of slaves as they struggled for freedom. In interviews and on questionnaires, these students indicated that they appreciated and enjoyed the opportunity to talk about these books, since they selected stories that were mostly about people with their same cultural heritage. There were so many choices of books in the classroom library that only one or two students had read the same book. The students seemed to relish the individual knowledge they had about their book (Thomas, 1980).

> It seems that most kids like the book talks. Most of the class was listening to the speakers. I think that part of its appeal is that the kids like to listen to each other. This is a case where kids have the knowledge as opposed to adults (teachers).
>
> (Observer's Notes, 12/9/91)

We believe that the African American students, and other students from minority cultures, experienced cultural validation when they read the literature and when they had the chance to talk about it as Karen describes here:

> *After the 15 minutes, we had book talks. I called on students who hadn't told the class about their books yet. Dianne talked about her book,* Secret of the Andes *(Clark, 1976). Reginald told about George Washington Carver. The students did an excellent job on these as always!*
>
> (Karen's Journal, 12/9/91)

Criterion 3: Student engagement in discussions about culturally relevant issues

The students responded positively to opportunities they were given to express their hostility toward oppressive conditions and prejudices against them due to their race or ethnicity and to describe some of their fears and worries about crime in their communities. According to Karen's journal and assisting observer data, more students participated with enthusiasm during this kind of discussion than during discussions that were less relevant to them:

> *The discussion about Dr. King was really good because several students were willing to share their knowledge of the circumstances of his death and their feelings about it. There was a lot of anger expressed, and the topic of the Ku Klux Klan was raised.*
>
> (Karen's Journal, 10/4/91)

In interviews and on questionnaires, the majority of African American students indicated a sense of validation toward their concerns and an appreciation for a teacher of a different racial background who was willing to listen and accept their feelings.

Discussion

The evidence we provided above of positive student responses to our alternative teaching strategies was primarily gleaned from the first two years of the study. However, in addition to documenting positive findings, we recognized obstacles among the less successful students which appeared to interfere with their effort and consequent achievement in the class. We discovered those obstacles as the result of analyzing all our data sources.

Consequently, even though we continued the third and fourth years of the study to examine issues related to the alternative teaching strategies, we were more focused on any factors which might intrude on our students' determination to earn "A's" and "B's" – grades they said they wanted and which we encouraged them to earn. We were mainly concerned with peer interactions which might decrease the students' motivation to be academically successful, and low grade tolerance even when the students had several opportunities to succeed. We were also looking for obstacles which might limit the academic self-confidence of our more "high-achieving" students such as the belief that they were receiving good grades only because of easy work rather than their ability, and the large number of high grades given in Karen's class which might lessen their value to the students. Hence, during the third and fourth years, the student questionnaires and surveys more closely matched these potential obstacles to success for the more "low-achieving" students and potential obstacles to increasing academic self-confidence for the more "high-achieving" students. These findings will be discussed in Chapter 7.

While the focus of the study may have shifted during the third and fourth years, we still were able to conclude, based on our classroom observation and student questionnaire and interview data, that the alternative teaching strategies were for the most part successful throughout all four years of the study.

Chapter 7

What gets in the way of student success?

Many of the students in this class seem motivated and enthusiastic about doing the work I give them. Their skills are pretty good. On the other hand, there are some students who seem very low-skilled and quietly resistant to doing the work. I will need to speak to them privately, warn them about getting work in, and send them to the tutoring center.

(Karen's Journal, 9/8/94)

Karen's reflections above – at the beginning of the third year of our study – express a common dilemma that teachers face. We knew from the first two years of our study that our alternative teaching strategies were successful with most of our students. However, we also discovered some unexpected obstacles to successful lessons and to the kind of academic performance we knew our students could achieve.

Unexpected obstacles – Years One and Two

During the first and second years of this study, there were some unexpected obstacles that got in the way of our goals. We began to address these in the second phase of our study – during the third and fourth years. One of the most critical obstacles involved the human element in the process of change: that is, the difficulties that teachers and their students have in accepting change – both in the curriculum and in themselves. They have these difficulties because they are human beings who have developed ways of thinking about themselves and have learned certain ways of doing things throughout their years in our school system.

Our contention is that since these difficulties with change are symptoms of teacher and student socialization in school, they must be anticipated and addressed from the outset if we seriously want to change the way schools serve all children. The evidence we report below includes difficulties with classroom discussions, student fear of failure, and students' familiarity and comfort with the "old ways of doing things."

Classroom discussions

One of the main obstacles with which Karen struggled concerned her own expectations of how discussions and small group projects should take place. She is a Caucasian, suburban woman who had taught mostly Caucasian, suburban students. The majority of students in her history classes during this study were African Americans from the inner city. Due to Karen's earlier experiences as a student and as a teacher, she was accustomed to conducting discussions in a certain way.

As each year progressed, Karen's students became more and more comfortable participating in class discussions, and she became more and more uncomfortable. Even though she encouraged participation, counting it as one quarter of the students' grade, Karen was expecting a certain kind of participation with the students raising their hands to be called on and commenting or answering in an orderly fashion – one at a time. When the students interacted freely, jumping into the discussion whenever an idea occurred to them, cutting off other students, getting louder and louder, Karen sometimes lost her patience and stopped the discussion. This frustrated the students because they felt that she was undermining their efforts to exchange ideas. Here is an excerpt from one of Karen's summaries which illustrates this struggle. The adult who is leading the discussion was the assisting observer that year who came to Karen's classroom twice each week:

> Diane talked to the class about the "Nation of Islam." Sonia, Desiree, and Charlene had lots to say. Dennis and Ralph carried on their own private conversation about Muhammed Ali, Malcolm X, and others. We finally gave up the discussion because it was out of control – but in a good way. Diane and I just can't handle that kind of discussion. Maybe teachers can

learn to deal with a more chaotic conversation – or should they?

(Karen's Journal, 2/24/92)

Here is a comment about Karen's difficulties handling discussions from a student during an interview with Diane at the end of the year. The student said: "No, we talk about it and she gets mad cause people get warmed up and she get mad. As soon as people start getting into it, she gets mad. No more discussion." The two boys being interviewed with her agreed and one of them added: "That's just how she do, man."

Diane asked: "Is there a better way to handle those discussions?" Their answers were: "Let us talk. Let us share our ideas." As much as Karen wanted to provide the students with thought-provoking, interactive, and supportive classroom experiences, her previous experience limited her tolerance for noise and chaotic exchanges. She virtually sabotaged potentially rich discussions. As well as facing her own difficulties because of earlier socialization, in working to change her students' perceptions of themselves as learners, Karen found that they too faced many similar unconscious obstacles.

Fear of failure

One student obstacle was a fear of failure. One type of fear was fear of sounding "dumb" during a discussion and being laughed at by classmates. Other fears had to do with writing poorly and having other students discover they could not read very well. Here are some excerpts from interviews with students during the first two years and from questionnaires in May 1992. The question asked was: Why do you think some people don't want to talk in class?

'Cause some people might say the wrong thing or something, and then, you know, and then people be laughing.

They might be laughed at and people might talk about you.

They don't want to ask because they don't want nobody to think they're dumb. They don't know how to do it, they won't just do it and get it all wrong, I ain't got to do this stuff, I be cool.

I don't have any ideas.

I think that people might make fun of me because I didn't have the right answer.

Familiarity with the old ways of doing things

Another obstacle was the students' familiarity with and ironic comfort with the "old ways of doing things" even though they had not been successful with those ways. One example of this was that, in the beginning of each year, the students connected good grades in the class to easy grading rather than to their ability. In a questionnaire toward the end of the first year (1990–1), one student said he felt smarter in Karen's class than in his other classes. When asked why, he wrote: "Because it's easy." Another student wrote: "The whole class can get an 'A' if they put their effort into their work." When asked the same question in the second year (1991–2), here are some ways students explained their higher grades in Karen's class: "'Cause it is easier"; "easy class, easy work"; and "the work is easy."

One explanation for this is that most of these students did poorly in elementary school and were getting low grades in their other classes at Mayfair so that they were not used to good grades and considered themselves to be poor students. As mentioned earlier, according to Weiner's attribution theory (1972, 1977), students who do poorly most of the time in school attribute success either to luck or to easy tasks instead of to a combination of effort and ability. Early in the year, as Weiner would have predicted, rather than attributing their better grades in Karen's class to their efforts and ability, her students attributed them mostly to her easy grading system. Later, however, they began to attribute them more to effort after continually experiencing success and hearing Karen attribute that success to their efforts.

The second example of the students' acceptance of "the old ways of doing things" relates to being given choice in their assignments and on other classroom experiences. Even though most of the students liked having a lot of choice in the class, there was some evidence that they perceived school as a place where they were supposed to follow orders and have decisions made for them. Here is how one student explained it in an interview at the end of the second year: "Why should you be able to choose? It's school." Another student was asked in an interview the second year how he would change what he learns in school and the way he does it. He answered: "Change it? You can't!"

These discrepancies – which we consider to be obstacles to change – between what teachers and students believe school should be like, as opposed to what they are familiar and comfortable with after years of socialization in the current system, are chasms that must be bridged in curriculum reform efforts. Otherwise there will be a continual, often subtle and unconscious, resistance to those efforts on the part of the students as well as the teachers, administrators, and parents.

Exploring potential obstacles: Years Three and Four

At the end of the first and second years of this study, even though many of our students received higher grades than in elementary school, we were not sure that higher grades necessarily meant improved self-confidence. We believed that improved self-confidence would help to sustain our students' motivation over the long run. Also, since we had noticed in those first two years that some students did not improve (even when Karen had worked hard to address the obstacles described at the beginning of this chapter), we were determined – in the third and fourth years, and with our students' help – to identify and address any additional obstacles that were interfering with their success. As we went into the third and fourth years of our study, then, one of our goals was to identify student perceptions of themselves and school that might be getting in the way of their academic self-confidence and high performance.

Obstacles to improved self-confidence

We looked at two obstacles which we thought might interfere with the academic self-confidence of our students who had improved grades. The two obstacles we explored were: perceived easy class and too many high grades. We speculated that if the successful students attributed their high achievement to an easy class and easy grading then their overall self-confidence might not improve.

Much to our surprise and delight, by the end of each year, our interview and questionnaire data indicated that all our students with improved grades attributed their success not to an easy class but to hard work and clear instructions. Also, they did not discredit their higher grades no matter how many other students received them as long as they believed they had earned them. Here are a few excerpts from interviews with our target students, conducted by the assisting observer between March and June of the third year which support these findings.

Interview 1

STUDENT: They understand what she means because she ain't like those teachers that talk faster and they can understand what she's saying, not asking her again to say it over.
INTERVIEWER: So you know the assignments?
STUDENT: Mm-hmm.
INTERVIEWER: How do you know them?
STUDENT: Because she helps us on them, and then when we go home, she ... then we already knew it.

Interview 2

INTERVIEWER: OK, the work seems easier because the students are getting better at it?
STUDENT A: It seems easier 'cause the teacher, she helps us do it faster and you can understand what she's doing, and you can understand how you do it and you need some help, you just call on her and she'll make you understand how it is.
STUDENT B: They believe that if they try their hardest, they can do better in class. It seems like they getting ... they like the work, and they start to get used to it, so it seems easier to do,

'cause the way they looking at it is like, "Well, this was too hard, this is too easy," so they like in between. But now the work is just ... at they pace.

Interview 3

STUDENT: I did all the work, and I listened.
INTERVIEWER: And that made you ...
STUDENT: Get better grades.
INTERVIEWER: And made you feel good about yourself?
STUDENT: Yeah ... I was doing all my work and then I understand it.
INTERVIEWER: So it made it seem easier to you?
STUDENT: Yeah.

Interview 4

INTERVIEWER: OK, who's responsible for the high grade you're getting?
STUDENT: Me.
INTERVIEWER: And how did you get it?
STUDENT: From working hard in class.

Interview 5

INTERVIEWER: So, you think the work was easy, and she graded easy, but you also said you worked hard – you were able to do work over, you could use your special talents, and you felt smart. So if the work's easy, how do you work hard?
STUDENT: Put more effort into doing it. Have fun with it, like doing it with friends, with partners. Doing different crafts with it. That's harder.
INTERVIEWER: Who's responsible for the higher grade you're getting? Did you earn it? Was the grade given to you? Did Mrs. Teel grade too easy? Was the work too easy?
STUDENT: I think I earned it.
INTERVIEWER: By ...

STUDENT: Working and showing Mrs. Teel what I knew how to do. What I was capable of doing. Such as the skit that I did that … the skit, that showed her what I was capable of doing.

Interview 6

INTERVIEWER: Why has your grade improved over the year?
STUDENT: I started doing my work more, and started paying attention in class.
INTERVIEWER: Anything else?
STUDENT: No.

Obstacles to "high student achievement"

Along with our concerns about obstacles in the way of our "high-achieving" students' improved self-confidence, our other concern was with obstacles to "high achievement" for the less successful students. There were two obstacles that we considered based on the literature about "low-achieving" African American students (Fordham and Ogbu, 1986) and also based on conversations with our students during the first two years of our study. These two obstacles were peer disapproval of high grades and what we are calling the "grade aspiration dilemma."

Peer disapproval of high grades

In their study in Stockton, California, Fordham and Ogbu (1986) found that African American high school students who excelled in their classes were harassed by their less successful peers. Because of their willingness to study hard and take school seriously, they were accused of selling out to the White establishment, thereby betraying their own culture and identities and "acting White". We speculated that our junior high school students might have some of the same peer pressures on them which could affect their motivation and high grade aspirations.

Once again, much to our surprise, our data during the third and fourth years of our study revealed that all of our students were proud of high grades and that they were not concerned about peer disapproval. In fact, all of them said that their peers didn't pay much attention to each other's grades. The one aspect of high achievement that they did comment on was the possibility of peer teasing or disapproval if they flaunted their high grades or acted superior because of them.

Here are some excerpts from interviews with our target students during the same time-period as the interviews above – between March and June of the third year.

Interview 1

INTERVIEWER: When you get good grades, does that make you feel awkward around your peers? Do they tease you about being a nerd? Or does it matter what they think, or how do you feel about it?

STUDENT: Not really, because if I'm getting good grades, I'm proud of myself, because I got the grades that I deserve. And I work for my A or my B. But instead, they're working for their D or their F. Instead of working for a A, B, or C.

Interview 2

INTERVIEWER: OK, when you get good grades does it ever make you feel awkward around your friends if you have good grades? Do they tease you?

STUDENT: No.

INTERVIEWER: Do they encourage you to get good grades? Your friends, not your family.

STUDENT: They don't care about my grades.

INTERVIEWER: They don't care about your grades?

STUDENT: No.

Interview 3

INTERVIEWER: OK, when your grade improved, were you worried about being teased by your friends about getting a good grade? Why or why not?

STUDENT: No, 'cause they … you get respect if you get good grades.

INTERVIEWER: Your friends would respect you?
STUDENT: Yeah.

Interview 4

INTERVIEWER: OK, do you think that a lot of students don't study so they'll be popular?
STUDENT: No.
INTERVIEWER: Would that be the same as being teased – you don't want to be teased, so you pretend you don't study, or … ?
STUDENT: No. Everybody, really, people don't get teased – they play around a lot, but they don't … they don't get teased.
INTERVIEWER: Your friends don't tease you about doing well?
STUDENT: No.
INTERVIEWER: Do most of your friends do well?
STUDENT: It's kind of half and half. (laughs)

Interview 5

INTERVIEWER: As your grade improved, and your grade really improved in this class, were you worried about being teased by your friends?
STUDENT: No. 'Cause it didn't really matter what they think.
INTERVIEWER: It doesn't matter what your friends think. OK. On the questionnaires, you said sometimes students tease other students who do well, but it doesn't bother you?
STUDENT: Mm-mm.
INTERVIEWER: If they tease you?
STUDENT: Mm-mm.
INTERVIEWER: Sometimes students don't study, to be popular, is that true?
STUDENT: No.
INTERVIEWER: That's not true?
STUDENT: Mm-mm.
INTERVIEWER: For you.
STUDENT: Mm-hmm. (laughs)
INTERVIEWER: It doesn't matter.
STUDENT: No.

INTERVIEWER: OK, so it doesn't matter at all if your friends tease you?

STUDENT: No.

(Student Interviews, 3/95–6/95)

As a result of collecting these kinds of interview data (and from the results of questionnaire data as well), during both the third and fourth years of our study, we ruled out peer disapproval of high grades as a potential obstacle to "high achievement". We began to concentrate instead on discrepancies between our students' grade aspirations and those of their parents or guardians and what they were willing to settle for in reality. In our data for both years, we found evidence of what we are calling a "grade aspiration dilemma".

Grade aspiration dilemma

When we got the results of the first quarter questionnaire (see Appendix C) that we administered in the third year (which asked our students questions about this issue), we were surprised once again (as we were with what we learned about the three potential obstacles – easy grading, too many high grades, and peer disapproval – described earlier). We discovered that every one of our students aspired to an "A" or "B" in Karen's class. We were surprised because we assumed that since many of our students had done poorly in upper elementary school that their grade aspirations – along with those of their parents or guardians – would have dropped from their earlier years in school. The other surprise (and disappointment), however, was that even with those high grade aspirations, some of our students (usually the ones who were receiving lower grades) said they would be proud and happy with a "C" and sometimes even with a "D". They indicated on the questionnaire that their parents or guardians would find those lower grades acceptable as well. They said that they would not get in trouble for receiving those lower grades – in some cases, only if they received an "F".

The gap between the desired grades and the acceptable grades is what we are calling the "grade aspiration dilemma." There have been a number of studies done that looked at the paradox between a positive student attitude toward education on the one hand and "low achievement" on the other (Carter, 1999;

MacLeod, 1987; Mickelson, 1990; Ogbu, 1994). These studies found that "low achieving," inner-city, African American high school students repeatedly stated that they valued education even though their academic performance was consistently below average ("D's" and "F's"). In these studies, the researchers explored possible explanations for this paradox, often attributing the "low achievement" to culturally inappropriate teaching strategies.

We believe that there are four distinct differences between those studies and ours. One difference is that Karen was working with junior high age students. Another difference is that Karen was not only a researcher in the classroom but was also the teacher. A third difference is that Karen was using culturally appropriate teaching strategies which she and her colleagues had designed based on motivation and school-failure literature. A fourth difference between this study and the earlier ones above is that we zeroed in on our students' specific grade aspirations. Our data clearly demonstrate high grade aspirations along with the contradictory attitude which allowed the students and their parents or guardians to "be okay" with much lower grades.

These data gave us unusual and very specific insight into the way our low-achieving students were thinking about their grades in Karen's class and the parallels between those students' perspectives on grades and that of their parents or guardians. This was a striking difference from most of the more "high-achieving" students who said that a "B" was the lowest grade that they and their parents or guardians would find acceptable. Some of these students were already making the connection between junior high grades and high school placement as seen in the excerpt below from an interview with a "high-achieving" student the third year:

> Um ... students want to do better, so it'll be ... it'll look good on your records, so when you go to the next school, they're like, "Oh, she's smart. Maybe she should go ... maybe she or he should go in a higher class or something" ... and they'll expect more from you, so they'll give you more.
>
> (Student Interview, 3/95)

Below is another example of the way the more "high-achieving" students think about the possibility of receiving "C's" or below in school. These differences in grade motivation among these students could partly explain the disparity in ultimate achievement levels. This interview took place at the end of the third year of our study:

INTERVIEWER: It also could be that if you know you worked really, really hard, and you still got a "B," if you had tried the best you could, if it was a real hard class, maybe not just Mrs. Teel's, but algebra or something like that?

STUDENT: And I got a "B"?

INTERVIEWER: Yeah.

STUDENT: I wouldn't really care, but my parents would.

INTERVIEWER: You wouldn't care? Ah ... that's interesting. A "B" is fine with you.

STUDENT: Yeah.

INTERVIEWER: A "C" wouldn't be?

STUDENT: No.

INTERVIEWER: But a "B" is OK?

STUDENT: A "C" is too low, 'Cause if you work hard in class, sometimes parents pay you for your grades. Like I do. If I get an "A", I get 5 bucks. Nothing for a "B".

INTEVIEWER: Nothing for a "C." Nothing for a "B"?

STUDENT: Nothing ... uh ... a lecture for a "B"; for a "C", probably "go to your room until dinner"; for a "D", "you're grounded" and for an "F" ... "you're dead."

(Student Interview, 6/95)

In contrast to the interview above, the student interviews below demonstrate the lower grade tolerance on the part of some of our "lower-achieving" students even when their grade aspirations were as high as the more "high-achieving" students. This "grade aspiration dilemma" may ultimately explain why, in Karen's class, these students, in the end, did not put in the effort it took to get the higher grades. The conversations took place during individual interviews conducted in the fourth year by the assisting observer in February, 1996:

Interview 1

INTERVIEWER: OK, on the questionnaire first quarter, you said
    you wanted a "B." You ended up with a "D," but you still
    said you were proud of that "D."
STUDENT: As long as I could pass.
INTERVIEWER: As long as you could pass. BUT you weren't happy
    that you got a "D." What was the reason you weren't happy?
STUDENT: I don't like "D's."
INTERVIEWER: You don't like "D's"?
STUDENT: Nuh-uh.
INTERVIEWER: "C's" are OK?
STUDENT: Yeah.
INTERVIEWER: But a "D" is better than an "F" so you'll pass?
STUDENT: Yeah.
INTERVIEWER: OK, thank you.

Interview 2

INTERVIEWER: First quarter, you wanted a "B", but you said you
    would accept an "F", and could still be proud of an "F".
    Second quarter, a "C," and the third quarter, you said you
    would still be proud of an "A" or a "B". So, earlier, if you
    wanted "A's" or "B's", how could you be proud of a "C" or
    even an "F"?
STUDENT: Long as I know I'm trying to do it.
INTERVIEWER: If you know you're trying, you could still be
    proud?
STUDENT: Mm-hmm.
INTERVIEWER: So what's the lowest grade you would be happy
    with?
STUDENT: A "C".

(Student Interviews, 2/96)

Discussion

As Karen identified these various obstacles over the course of the
study, she modified her teaching approach. Before we collected the
questionnaire and interview data which revealed the "grade
aspiration dilemma," she responded to incomplete assignments
with the same consequences she had always used. The first year,

Karen encouraged her students to finish the assignments or to re-do them for a higher grade. In the second year, she also called home to ask the students' parents or guardians to talk to them about the missing work. At that time, however, Karen did not have a clear idea as to her students' or their families' grade aspirations so she did not put a great deal of pressure on them to complete their assignments.

During the third year of the study, when our data revealed the "grade aspiration dilemma," Karen's response to incomplete assignments changed dramatically. Hence, the strategies Karen used to deal with her "low-achieving" students evolved over time. The stages in her responses to unsatisfactory performance – as she learned more about her students' aspirations – are described in Chapter 8.

Taking on the role of detective

Teacher's response to struggling students

> Today, I felt like maybe I am coddling the students too much in asking them to do a better job on their drawings, but I feel like I should expect them to do their very best and then insist that they do when they don't!! I will call some more homes tonight.
>
> (Karen's Journal, 10/26/95)

Karen's notes above – written during the fall of the fourth year of our study – indicated a shift compared to the first year in her approach with the "lower-achieving" students. During the later years of the study, instead of encouraging the students as a group to do their best and then leaving them on their own, Karen became more aggressive in her determination to promote the success of *all* her students. She decided that she needed to consistently put more pressure on them, as she mentions in her notes above. She began talking with individual students privately during class time, calling home more often, assigning after-school work sessions, and eventually focusing on their college and career aspirations.

As we reflected back on the approach toward unsatisfactory academic performance that Karen used over all four years of our study, we realized that her strategies evolved in four stages as she responded to her "low-achieving" students. The four stages were: Stage One, Year One – belief in the students and alternative teaching strategies; Stage Two, Year Two – belief in the students, alternative teaching strategies, and more home contact; Stage Three, Year Three – belief in the students, alternative teaching strategies, more home contact, and before- and after-school work sessions; and, finally, Stage Four, Year Four – belief in the students, alternative teaching strategies, more home contact, before- and after-school work sessions, and focus on college and career.

Karen's stages of promoting success

Stage One, Year One: Belief in the students; alternative teaching strategies

When we designed the alternative teaching strategies in the graduate seminar, we believed at that time, as mentioned earlier, that offering such experiences to Karen's students would be enough motivation and support for each one of them to work toward "A's" and "B's." We believed in the intelligence and abilities of the students and assumed that giving more diverse assignments would tap into their individual strengths and talents, and that each one of them would grab the opportunity to improve their grade. As we have mentioned before, the students were encouraged to re-do poor work and to turn in work late with a moderate penalty. Here is an excerpt from a student's question-naire in the spring of the first year, in which he describes how he felt in Karen's classroom given the environment she was trying to create:

> I liked a lot of it, really how we read in class. I liked that the class was relaxing and it was fun to learn about history in a nice environment I look forward to coming to the class.
>
> (Student Questionnaire, 4/30/91)

Unfortunately, just because many of the students expressed a certain comfort level in Karen's class, that didn't mean that they were motivated to complete all the assignments. Even when we thought we had created a particularly interesting assignment, many of them either turned it in late or not at all. This attitude and behavior puzzled us.

At that time, during the first year of our study, Karen had clear consequences for nonconformist behavior on the part of her students, based exclusively on the class rules. However, there were no consequences for incomplete work apart from constant reminders in class from Karen to the students as a group and a "C", "D", or "F" report card grade at the end of the quarter. Every once in a while during that first year, Karen called home if a student wasn't cooperating in class, wasn't on time, or was absent a lot. Typically, before discussing these more negative issues, Karen talked to the parents or guardians about their child's strengths and talents that she had observed. Apart from that kind of phone call, however, Karen did not put any additional pressure on her students with regard to their academic behavior. We were hoping such pressure would not be necessary.

At the end of that first year of our study, though, we noticed that even when many of Karen's students had very similar skill levels, several factors appeared to make a difference for the "high-achieving" students. These factors were: their attendance in class, how well they followed through on assignments, and their unwillingness to accept a grade lower than a "B" like the "high-achieving" student described in Chapter 7. Those students who consistently earned "C's" appeared to accept that mediocre grade, even though there were opportunities for them to revise their work and improve their grade. Here is a description of a group interview at the end of the first year when the students being interviewed explain why assignments are either turned in just before the end of the quarter or sometimes even overlooked:

> One reason kids might turn their work in is because it's the end of the grading period and time for progress reports and they want a higher grade. They will even ask for extra credit. Kids don't do homework because they like to watch television, play Nintendo, and just forget about it. They then go to school, and may try to do it during class. Franklin says that he does it as the teacher is going over the answers. They claim that they wouldn't do more homework if they had it. Students tell their parents varying stories about homework when asked. Parents seem to believe what the kids tell them.
>
> (Student Group Interview, 6/13/91)

We were disappointed that some of Karen's students did not work up to their ability and realized that something more needed to be done to convince them to complete all of their work. This led Karen to stage two.

Stage Two, Year Two: More home contact

One of the decisions that the seminar participants made at the end of the first year about the next year was to make more contact with the students' families. The experiences, though infrequent, with family contact in the first year had been extremely positive and productive in terms of student motivation for many of our students. The families were concerned and supportive. They especially appreciated hearing compliments about their children. As mentioned earlier, when Karen talked to a family member, she always described the student's strengths and areas where he or she could improve. This turned out to be a very effective approach, but we realized that Karen hadn't used it enough.

During the second year of our study, Karen made phone calls home on a more regular basis, talking primarily with the parents or guardians of the "low-achieving" students. As in the first year, Karen shared her perceptions of the students' strengths and potential. She also asked them to talk to their children about their late and missing work, and she asked about any recent absences. In an interview conducted at the end of the second year, when a student was asked to describe Karen, he said: "She takes time to help students, cares about students, and calls their parents" (Student Interview, 6/92).

Our purpose that second year was to develop a strong team relationship between Karen and the parents or guardians where they worked together toward improving the achievement of her students. Here is an excerpt from the assisting observer's notes during the second year about the positive impact of home contact on one student's attitude toward class:

> I had a talk with Ronnie before he left for the library. He was reading an Agatha Christie book. I pointed out that those books were famous and asked him what it was about. He told me. I told him that I was glad to see him reading such a book because I knew that he was an excellent reader. He was pleased. He added that Karen had called his home and he had "kind of eavesdropped." He heard Karen tell his mother that he was the best reader in the class. He said that he was happy to hear that. He added that Karen said that he needed to work on talking in class and finishing his work. I encouraged him to work on those two areas. It was clear that hearing that he was a good reader made a difference for Ronnie. I don't know if

he always read books like Agatha Christie novels, but it struck me as a higher level book than he usually chooses. I wonder if that is related to a newfound confidence in his reading ability. This example shows, in a way, how powerful positive phone calls can be, not only for parents, but for kids as well.

(Observer Notes, 3/16/92)

This additional home contact was helpful in bringing about improvements in Karen's students' behavior in class, but had very little impact on missing work. We were realizing that Karen needed to apply much more pressure on her students in terms of following through on their assignments. Karen now believed that by enforcing more strict consequences for incomplete work, her students would complete more work and begin to live up to her high expectations for them. This was when Karen moved to stage three.

Stage Three, Year Three: Before- and after-school work sessions for unfinished assignments

When we were planning for the second phase of the study (years three and four), we decided, based on our experiences in years one and two, that some of Karen's students would not always complete assignments unless she pressured them into it. More home contact had made a difference for some students, but not for all of them. Karen decided to assign before- and after-school work sessions for students who were not completing their work.

She believed that her students with missing or below average work might become motivated to apply themselves more seriously knowing that, if not, they would be required to come in for these extra work sessions. She didn't want to "let them get away" with average or below average work when we knew they were capable of much more. As mentioned in Chapter 6, some of the students simply weren't applying themselves when given the choice even though their grade aspirations were as high as the more "high-achieving" students. Karen wanted to take the option of not doing the work away from them, since we knew (even if they did not) that average grades and below would put them on a track in school that could preclude them from many college and job opportunities.

Also, after learning (from our questionnaire data at the beginning of year three) that *all* of Karen's students had high grade aspirations, we felt there was especially strong justification to apply more pressure on each and every one of them to excel.

Here is an excerpt from an individual student interview early in the third year of our study where the student gives his impression of Karen's before- and after-school work session policy:

INTERVIEWER: All teachers want you to do the best and succeed, and Mrs. Teel knows you were disappointed in your grade this quarter. If there are teachers that are getting you to do your work, what are they doing? What makes the difference? How does a teacher like Mrs. Teel get you to do the work?

STUDENT: She has confidence in you. She knows you could do it. That's why she keeps pressuring you. She writes your name on the board to stay after school and stuff. 'Cause she wants you to get a good grade. She knows people don't care about theirself, but she care about people.

(Student Interview, 11/94)

These extra work sessions turned out to be very successful for some of these students because often they either did not understand the assignment or just needed a little encouragement to plod through it. Probably even more important was the one-on-one attention that was possible between the students and Karen before or after school. This time spent together helped to strengthen their relationship, and they began to respect and understand each other better and to communicate more effectively as well. After spending this kind of quality time with the students, Karen felt that she knew them better and was better able to support their needs. This led to an ever-improving rapport with the students.

In the excerpt below from one of our many student interviews during this third year of our study, Richard, one of our target students, comments on his developing rapport with Karen. In this chapter, we frequently refer to Richard. He is an excellent example of the many bright and capable students in Karen's classes over the years who continued to be "low achievers" despite Karen's efforts to guide them in *making school count*.

INTERVIEWER: Why do you think you just do better here?

RICHARD: 'Cause she always tells us to do our work and come in after school and finish ... and she's one of the nicest teachers I got so far – the rest is always kicking me out.

INTERVIEWER: (laughs)

RICHARD: So ... that's why I always do good in this class.

(Student Interview, March 1995)

As a result of more home contact during the second and third years and before- and after-school work sessions in the third year, we found that Karen's students' behavior improved. They were more respectful toward one another and toward Karen, and most students were tardy and absent less than they had been before Karen applied these pressures.

Unfortunately, during each of those years, even after coming to several before- or after-school work sessions with Karen, there was a group of students who consistently received average grades and below because they had missing and/or poor quality assignments. At the end of the fourth quarter of the third year of our study, eighteen out of twenty-five students received "A's" and "B's" while six received "C's", no one received a "D", and one received an "F". This was indeed a major improvement over the first quarter, when only thirteen students had "A's" and "B's", three had "C's", and nine received "D's". However, there were still seven very capable students who were not taking advantage of their opportunity to excel in school and achieve their aspirations, even though each of them expressed the kind of support for Karen's before- and after-school work sessions policy as Richard did in the interview above.

At this point, at the end of the third year of our study, Karen decided that believing in the students, offering them an alternative classroom environment, making more home contact, and assigning before- and after-school work sessions were still not adequate strategies to promote high academic achievement for all her students.

What Karen had experienced thus far was disappointing, since she was not able to reach some of her students, as she discusses in these excerpts from her notes during the third year:

It takes a great deal of patience and determination on the part of teachers to keep on students who are clearly not doing their best and to be in touch with their families. It seems that students have to be aware of a pay-off for them that comes from extra effort. If they don't think that pay-off is there, they seem to shut down ahead of time and to do the bare minimum.

(Karen's Journal, 1/30/95)

Still struggling to find a way to get all *of the students to do their work so their grade doesn't suffer. I still don't have the magic formula, but sometimes the kids really work and other times they seem to loaf. I'll keep trying different approaches.*

(Karen's Journal, 3/31/95)

As a teacher researcher, Karen thought of herself as a detective, trying to solve a mystery, looking for the missing links in her strategies with her students as she expresses at the end of the third year:

Putting pressure on my students to do work doesn't always succeed. It can be very discouraging for me, and what I need to do is to find out more about this resistance. Also, I would like to find out from the target students what does *work with them. Each student is so different with different histories, pressures at home, and personalities. It's just so hard to know which kind of strategy to use when I know so little really about each student.*

(Karen's Journal, 6/8/95)

As a result of that perception of herself as a teacher researcher, even when the strategies she used in years one through three were not as successful as she wanted, and even when she had experiences like the ones she describes below, Karen still believed that she could identify some missing "piece of the puzzle" that might make the difference with the remaining "low-achieving" students like Richard – as she expresses in her notes below:

Richard came in late but an outreach person had been looking for him so I felt I should send Richard up to talk with him. It was frustrating, though, because when I get him in class I want to keep him there!! Even though I talked to Michael's Dad yesterday, he was not in class today again. His Dad told me he would be there today. He said he was late to school yesterday because he had a nose bleed from an allergy attack. There is always some excuse. I just don't know what to do about Michael and Richard. Today I talked with an African American support person, and he said he thinks the reason that there are major achievement discrepancies is because of the parents or guardians. He said if they don't care or if they don't have their act together enough to push their children, then the students will not do what they need to do to succeed. I asked him if he thought there was anything we could do as a school. He said that over the years he has become convinced that the kids who live with "messed up" families are just not going to respond at school. They don't have the guidance and incentive to put out the effort required to do well. We were talking in the hall for a few minutes. It was kind of a discouraging exchange, but I still think there are things we can do as a school to try and encourage the students (no matter what their life circumstances are) to try their best. We shall see ...

(Karen's Journal, 4/95)

At this point in the study, Karen decided to pay more attention to students like Richard who were consistently earning "C's" or lower. Despite their desire for "A's" and "B's", they were apparently willing to settle for these lower grades. We knew that even though these students were doing better than they had before in school, by settling for average grades or below they were seriously limiting their college and career opportunities. They were not making the extra effort required to produce higher quality work even when they had choices within assignments and were given many chances to improve. This behavior indicated to us that Karen's students might not fully understand the importance of high grades for high school class placement (Oakes, 1985) and for college admission and the careers that would follow (Leondari *et al.*, 1998).

We decided that Karen needed to commit much more time and energy inside and outside the classroom, to trying to convince the "lower-achieving" students and their families to think of those "A's" and "B's" as "critical keys" to attaining their high school, college, and career aspirations. This shift in thinking led Karen to Stage Four.

Stage Four, Year Four: Focus on college and career

At the same time as Karen was beginning to think more about the students' college and career aspirations, during the fourth year of our study, she continued to assign work sessions before and after school and to put pressure on those students with incomplete assignments. Here she comments on that approach:

> *I'm concerned about some of the students getting further and further behind. There are still some students who haven't finished their state reports. I have to keep giving them work sessions and calling home until they get all their work in.*
>
> (Karen's Journal, 10/11/95)

As with the student response during the third year, assigning work sessions was not always effective with the students in the beginning of the fourth year, as Karen reflects in these notes:

> *I'm still puzzled by how many students are not turning in their work even when I give them work sessions. Are they just being difficult, rebellious, etc. or are they really forgetting or just don't have that future orientation that might motivate them to complete less than exciting assignments. Are they bored or would they still not hand in homework that they found really interesting?*
>
> (Karen's Journal, 10/27/95)

> *Even my giving the students after-school work sessions and calling home didn't help with certain students. They were absent too much and pretty lethargic during class time. Yet, each one says they want to do well.*
>
> (Karen's Journal, 11/3/95)

Also during the fourth year, Karen continued to ask her students to answer questions about their grade aspirations along with those of their parents or guardians. As we mentioned in Chapter 7, each quarter our data revealed that all the students wanted "A's" and "B's" in Karen's class, and that they believed that their parents or guardians wanted them to earn those grades as well. Most students were responding well to the pressures that Karen was putting on all of them to do their best, and she continually provided praise and positive feedback for successful efforts. However, there were still students who were not completing their work as well as they could have. Here is an excerpt from Karen's notes during December of the fourth year in which she continues to ponder the "grade aspiration dilemma" of some of her students:

> I seem to be stuck on those who are not performing well and trying to get insight into that problem. I also keep coming back to the question of what is causing the major and wide-spread discrepancy between student grade aspirations and the grade they actually get which they are often proud of anyway.
> (Karen's Journal, 12/13/95)

Karen began experimenting during the fourth year, often successfully, with several different strategies which emphasized the connection between junior high grades and college and career goals. We hoped that these strategies would eliminate the gap between the students' and their parents' or guardians' desire for "A's" and "B's" and their acceptance of "C's" and "D's" – an attitude we felt was hurting their chances for success in school.

With this approach, Karen tried the following strategies. She started talking to her students in class on a regular basis and frequently communicating with the students' families over the phone and in school meetings about the crucial link between grades in junior high and high school and their college and career aspirations. Here is an example of an occasion when Karen used this new strategy:

> After school today, Richard's mother came in for a conference with his teachers. We met in my room. I had brought my Dad's old alarm clock for Richard, since his mom had told me over the phone that she was the only one in the house with an alarm clock and sometimes she oversleeps. I repeated what I had said several times over the phone. Richard is smart and very capable, but he is absent way too much. I talked to them both about the future and about how important grades are – like the keys to the future. I told Richard that whether he is bored or not, he must do the work and get good grades so he will get what HE wants down the road. Richard said he

wanted to be in sports as a career. We talked about the different possibilities.

(Karen's Journal, 1/23/96)

Each time she talked to either the students or family members as Karen did with Richard and his mother, she would talk about the students' strengths and accomplishments in her class. She also worked at enlisting the parents or guardians to join her in putting more pressure on the students to get their work done. Here is an example of how strongly Karen was beginning to feel about implementing this approach:

I'm just more convinced than ever that I need to stay on these kids both in class and over the phone when they aren't coming to school or aren't completing the work. The support from home is tremendous WHEN THEY KNOW! I feel like the parents or guardians get a very strong message from me too though about how serious I am about their child succeeding in my class!!

(Karen's Journal, 1/26/96)

In February of the fourth year, it occurred to Karen that in her more recent notes she was describing her contact with the students and with their families outside class more and more. She realized that an observer, when assessing the class experience, would not be aware of these other, sometimes more critical moments between Karen and her students and their families. Here are her reflections on that situation:

I am realizing more and more how much I am dealing with outside of the classroom where the reality of these students' lives is pulling away from their dreams and my dreams inside the classroom. As I look over my notes, I see that I am describing what goes on outside of the actual classroom experience between me and the students and their families – experiences that a classroom observer is unaware of. So the classroom life is almost an aberration because it's not the whole story. There is a reality to the school experience that is seldom discussed and rarely written about to my knowledge. I see myself shifting in my focus and coming to understand how important it is for teachers to promote a blend of that reality outside and the reality inside to somehow bring them together. It just isn't happening for lots of kids.

(Karen's Journal, 2/2/96)

In addition to reflecting on her increasing contact with the students and their families outside class, Karen was thinking more and more about how some students seemed so much more distracted by their circumstances outside class than other students did. Here is an excerpt from Karen's notes during the fourth year in which she shows her frustration:

I really struggled today to keep the students with me. I feel such competition on some days with the things that distract them from the lesson. It really does seem like we teachers must offer them novel, interesting tasks that will draw them in. Their outside interests are of such keen interest to some of them. I guess my big question is why. Why are some kids so easily distracted from the lesson while others can stay focused no matter how boring the activity might be considered. There's a switching of gears that goes on for some students from the outside to the inside of classrooms. For others that gear switching does not happen. I'll keep thinking about this ...

(Karen's Journal, 2/8/96)

The before- and after-school work sessions actually started to have a positive impact as the year progressed. Here is what one student had to say about this policy:

INTERVIEWER: Does Mrs. Teel's class encourage you more than other classes? Does she encourage you to get your work in, to keep your grades up, to think you can do more?

STUDENT: Yeah, she encourages more than to bring homework in. She encourages more because she puts more pressures on us because she'll give us after-school work sessions if we don't. And that puts more pressure. And in other classes, they just, if you don't do it, they just give you a bad grade. So she does pressure me more than any of my other classes.

(Student Interview, 4/96)

Even though more and more students – like the one in the interview above – attested to the positive impact of Karen's before-and after-school work session policy, throughout the fourth year she continued to search for additional strategies that might make a difference for her students who were still lagging behind. Toward the end of the fourth year, she administered a new questionnaire to the students (see Appendix D). That questionnaire, in addition to asking them questions about school-connected skills, asked them about their interests outside school and about their college and career aspirations. Karen had decided to become familiar with her students' individual college and career interests, and, on a regular basis, to work at showing them the link between high grades in school and those college and career aspirations. In this way, she thought, the students would see an especially compelling rationale for working toward and earning top grades. Here is an excerpt from Karen's notes in which she shares her excitement and hope regarding this new approach:

> *I was excited about finding out what each student is thinking about for a career. I think once I find out what the students' goals are I can connect more effectively with them. My knowledge of each one of them will be so much broader, and, as I've said before, I can tap into that knowledge to motivate them – I hope.*

> (Karen's Journal, 4/24/96)

We were all surprised once again at how high all of the students' college and career aspirations were. As with the "low-achieving" students' responses about their grade aspirations, we had assumed that because of so many years of average or below average teacher evaluations, that the "lower-achieving" students' college and career goals would have become quite modest and limited. This was not the case. The students expressed an interest in top universities such as Harvard, University of California at Berkeley, and Stanford. They also told us that they were aspiring toward such professions as law, medicine, education, business, and music.

Here are some examples of what the students said:

Interview 1

INTERVIEWER: What do you see yourself doing in 10 years?

STUDENT: I'll be home in Mississippi, going to college.

INTERVIEWER: How will you get there?

STUDENT: I'll walk. (laughs)

INTERVIEWER: You'll walk? (laughs) How will you get to college? How important are your grades in school for getting into college?

STUDENT: They're very important, 'cause I've already been recommended to Mississippi State – I had to do a survey in the sixth grade, and they wanted to know how you were ... what activities you were in, like a brief application of what you were doing then. And I was recommended to go there, so ... My grades would definitely have to be up for me to go home, 'cause my parents already told me if my grades weren't up, I was gonna stay out here, and I don't want to stay out here. I want to go home. So I have to keep my grades up.

INTERVIEWER: OK, what kind of career do you want, once you're through college?

STUDENT: I want to be a travelling nurse.

INTERVIEWER: A travelling nurse?

STUDENT: You travel in different countries ... you travel like every other ... 3 months. Or, maybe basketball. I want to play basketball. But my mom told me, she said we make more money – women make more money being nurses than they do playing basketball.

(Student Interview, 5/96)

Interview 2

INTERVIEWER: What do you see yourself doing in 10 years from now?

STUDENT: I'll probably ... 10 years? I want to be a chemist. Because I like science. And I think I'll be a chemist.

INTERVIEWER: You think you'll be a chemist? OK. And so in 10 years, you want to be a chemist – how do you plan to get there? Do you know what you need to do?

STUDENT: Uh-huh – I need to take a lot of ... I need to take ... can you take chemistry more than one time in high school?

INTERVIEWER: I think they have advanced chemistry if you do well.

STUDENT: I'll try to take 2 years of chemistry and then when I go to college, I'll know what to do, since I took advanced chemistry, and then I'll just ... and then after college, I'll try to apply for a job to be a chemist.

INTERVIEWER: What do you see ... as a chemist, working for a corporation like Chevron or ...

STUDENT: Yeah, Chevron.

(Student Interview, 5/96)

Once we became aware of the students' high college and career aspirations which did not correlate with the "grade aspiration dilemma," described earlier, we concluded that the alternative teaching strategies, calls home, and before- and after-school work sessions were not enough incentive for some of our students to work for the "A's" and "B's" to which they aspired.

Karen noted these college and career interests on her seating chart, began to refer to those interests on a regular basis in class, and built them into the curriculum as much as possible. By implementing these new ideas, Karen was attempting to convince her students and their families of the critical connection between the students' grades in school and their college and career aspirations. Karen started referring to that connection with the students both publicly and privately, and we developed some additional strategies which we hoped would promote that connection as well.

For example, in addition to the way she referred to the students' college and career aspirations on her seating chart, during calls to the students' homes, and during conferences with parents or guardians, Karen also began – toward the end of the fourth year – to incorporate the students' career interests into the curriculum. For example, during a unit on the Civil War, if any student expressed an interest in teaching, Karen encouraged them to do research on a teacher during that time. If the student was African American, she expected that person to find out about an African American teacher during those times. If the student wanted to be a police person, Karen told them to read about law enforcement during the Civil War.

These strategies served as motivators for the students' completion of their assignments. Most students appeared engaged in the tasks. Karen started using this last strategy fairly late in the fourth year of our study. Because of that timing, we have very little data on its impact. Karen's observation notes tell us, however, that the students began to make the connection between their interests and the curriculum Karen was using with them.

As part of this strategy to encourage the students to connect the subject matter with their career interests, Karen arranged for one of her African American students, Michelle, to go with her to the University of California at Berkeley to interview a historian about African American teachers in the years preceding the Civil War. Michelle's career aspiration was to become a teacher, and she wanted to attend the University of California at Los Angeles. She had started out the year receiving "C's", "D's", and "F's" in Karen's classes, similar grades to the ones she received in upper elementary school. At this point, late in the year, she was earning a "B+" in Karen's class. She had prepared questions for the historian, and she taped the interview. Among other stories, the historian told Michelle about free African American women from the North who would come to southern plantations and pretend to teach sewing while actually teaching the slaves to read. Michelle wrote a report about this story with illustrations.

Karen's students responded very positively to this latest strategy, although for a few of them the timing appeared to be too late. They had stopped coming to school or were arriving at Karen's class halfway through the period or toward the end, and could not work on assignments effectively. Karen eventually learned that there were distractions for these students outside school that she and the other teachers could not compete with at this point. Even though these same students had clearly expressed an interest in success in school, their motivation had moved to a different arena. Here is an excerpt from Karen's notes in which she reflects on this dilemma, focusing again on Richard:

> I talked to one of our support personnel after class. He told me that he had seen Richard at the BART station yesterday around fourth period, smoking and shooting dice. He had been in my class first period and did some work. It's discouraging to know how strong the pull is for Richard away from school. What can we do for students like him to make school more relevant and appealing?
>
> (Karen's Journal, 3/21/96)

As Karen became more aware of the circumstances that were keeping her students from doing their best in school, she made it her mission for the remainder of the year to explore strategies that would help her students make the connection between their classroom grades and their college and career aspirations. We believe that if every teacher would focus on these connections with all their students and emphasize those connections early in school and as often as possible, then students like Richard might be better able to concentrate on their studies and to resist those forces that so often compete with the classroom experience and which lead to "low achievement."

Chapter 9

Turning student aspirations into realities

> If the future is an achievement ... then teachers are futurists along with politicians, filmmakers, and journalists – those individuals who according to J. McClellan (1978) "make other people's futures more real to them." Indeed, at its best, education should provide students with a sense of empowerment that makes the future "real" by moving beyond merely offering children plausible alternatives to indicating how their preferred dreams can actually be attained.
>
> (Covington, 1992: 3)

The key question we asked in the original seminar was why, from an academic standpoint, are so many inner-city African American students having trouble in our nation's schools? Why are so many students doing poorly in school when we know they are capable of learning? Over and over again in the literature on urban school failure, which inspired this work, clear evidence is presented which demonstrates that inner-city, African American students are intelligent, capable, and motivated young people who excel in oral, narrative, artistic, organizational, imaginative, and creative skills. The data collected and analyzed in this four-year study support this literature. Yet, many of these students – with all of that potential – end up doing poorly in our nation's schools.

African American students continue to be placed in "slow groups" in elementary school and in the lowest tracked classes in junior high and high school. There is a major incongruence in this testing and placement pattern where bright, capable students are considered to be incapable of high achievement.

The classroom approach in this study was developed so that Karen could try to counteract the pattern of school failure among inner-city, African American students in her classroom. We were convinced that, even if her students had received poor assessments in elementary school, they might respond in a positive way if Karen created an equitable environment for them. As we described in Chapter 6, given a non-competitive, supportive classroom environment in which multiple abilities were recognized and improvement was rewarded, many of these "at-risk" students showed positive gains in attitude, behavior, and academic performance by the end of the year. For example, there were more students at the end of each year who spoke up in discussions, who completed high-quality writing assignments, and who were reading with more interest and stronger skills than they had demonstrated at the beginning of the year.

This improvement resulted from two major factors. One factor was that, by and large, they earned good grades from Karen – especially compared to their grades in upper elementary school and compared to their other classes in seventh grade. They received better grades because they were graded on several criteria such as speaking, listening, reading, writing, leadership, cooperation, creativity, imagination, and artwork. The other factor responsible for their improvements in attitude, behavior, and performance was the constant reminders both to the students and to their families of Karen's expectations and belief in their abilities.

As part of our collaboration early in this study, the seminar participants often discussed the students' self-doubts and lowered motivation as demonstrated in their resistance to writing and to participation in discussions, and in disruptive behavior. We designed new lessons and teaching strategies or modified the old ones, hoping to address these difficulties. Karen continued to wrestle with these issues each year as a teacher researcher, hopefully working toward a better understanding of her "low-achieving" students. That is the best way we knew of to serve the needs of these students more effectively and break the cycle of school failure for them.

Given the findings of this four-year study, there are several implications for teaching, for school/university and in-school collaboration, and for teacher education. In the remainder of this chapter, we will explore these implications.

Implications for teaching

> If we want these students to value education they must be shown
> that they can succeed at education.
>
> (Marchant, 1990: 14)

The findings from the type of classroom research represented in
this book have definite implications for teaching. As Marchant
(1990) asserts above, it seems clear that teachers should make it
possible for their students to succeed – for them to get "A's" and
"B's" in their classes. "Low-achieving" students will never believe
in their ability to succeed in school and they will never have
enough confidence as students to persevere in difficult times if
they have never known success. All Karen's students had strengths
for which she gave them credit as much as possible. All teachers
should celebrate their students' diverse strengths, talents, and
cultural backgrounds in various ways in their classroom approach,
in order to validate their students and in doing so promote their
success.

These students also need guidance in class discussions and in
group work. We found repeatedly that they do not automatically
know how to engage in these activities. Also, the students need
structured, clearly defined lessons with some choice and flexibility
built into them. In addition, improvement in reading and writing
skills is critical for these students to succeed. However, teachers
need to come up with creative and diverse classroom experiences
which will motivate their students to improve in those areas.
Finally, teachers should allow their students to take on more
responsibility in the running of the class to build self-esteem and
trust between them. All teachers should *listen* to their students
much more than is probably common.

When looking at the educational importance of this study, there
are three particularly salient conclusions: (1) taking school-failure
theories into account when planning a teaching approach appears
to be valuable; (2) the use of innovative methods, such as a non-
competitive classroom structure, motivates positive academic
performance by most students at risk of school failure; and (3) the
use of non-traditional activities in the teaching of World History,
such as role-playing and reading historical fiction, appears to
promote increased interest, learning, and understanding.

Finally, one of the most critical factors in the future success of these students is the nature of the expectations teachers have for them – the kind of "classroom heritage" that permeates the environment experienced by the students on a daily basis. Unless *all* students are expected to earn "A's" and "B's" and are not allowed to settle for lower grades, those who "are allowed" to become "low achievers" will not be in a position to compete with more "high-achieving" students for college admission and for professional careers.

These high expectations for academic success for every student should be a *dominant* feature of the school environment in every teacher's classroom and as part of other school-wide programs and activities. All students should learn about the college and career opportunities available to them, and what the academic expectations are. They should also have practice *during school time* in taking the tests required for college admission such as the Scholastic Aptitude Test (SAT). We have become convinced that providing students with an academically and culturally supportive environment *and* emphasizing this college and career connection on a regular basis in schools are critical strategies to promoting success more effectively, *making school count* for all students.

In reflecting on all the issues that came to light during the four years of this research, we have developed a set of eight essential components that we believe should be an integral part of every teacher's classroom. These are components that are different from subject matter because they address and support each student individually on several different levels. We present these eight essential components in an acronym, "CREATIVE." Each letter of the word "CREATIVE" represents one of the eight components.

We suggest that teachers incorporate the eight components described below into their strategies and curriculum. The eight components are: Cultural Awareness, Reading and Writing Skills, Effort, Aspirations, Talent, Interests, Variety, and Excellence.

C = Cultural awareness

Recognize the uniqueness and importance of all cultures. Allow students to explore their own cultures through reading materials available to them and through activities which give them the opportunity to honor their backgrounds. Learn as much as possible about the culture of each student in your classes in order to be a more effective teacher for all of your students.

R = Reading and writing skills

Emphasize reading and writing in your curriculum because it is essential that our students develop strong skills in those areas. If you have a computer lab at your school, spend as much time there as possible with your classes, working on developing those skills, since our students enjoy computers very much and do not necessarily have access to them.

E = Effort

Recognizing effort and mastery as important criteria for success builds student confidence in their ability to succeed and encourages them to persevere. If students are always compared to each other rather than against designated requirements, those students who take longer to fulfill the requirements may become discouraged and may stop trying.

A = Aspirations

Student college and career aspirations can be very useful if teachers are aware of them and use them throughout their curriculum to motivate their students to do their best. Schools should emphasize the future in terms of college and career goals and inform all students about the opportunities available to them and how to reach their goals. In addition, teachers and administrators should familiarize the students with the various forms of financial assistance that are available to them. This strategy is extremely important, since some of our students have the incorrect impression that they cannot find financial support. As a result, many of them do not aim for college.

T = Talent

Each student has unique talents with which teachers should be familiar, and they should encourage their students to use them in completing assignments. If students are allowed to shine, using their own, special talents, their confidence to take risks in other areas will improve.

I = Interests

All students have individual interests that can be incorporated into assignments as motivators. The more interested in the topic the students are, the more willing they will be to complete whatever tasks they are given.

V = Variety

When students are given choices in their assignments, they feel a sense of agency. The more variety there is in the kinds of assignments the students are asked to complete, the more interested they will be.

E = Excellence

Above all, when teachers give their students assignments, they should emphasize high standards. Teachers should hold their students to those standards but give them more than one chance to reach them.

All these ideas for strategies that we developed over the course of our study were the result of collaboration among academics, teachers, and students. Our findings offer clear implications for collaboration between schools and universities, among the faculty and staff at the school site, and between teachers and their students.

Implications for collaboration

School–university collaboration

Though our classroom experiences sometimes fell short of our expectations during the four years of this research, the camara-derie of our collaborative group and our commitment to supporting each other and the students made us rely on our respective areas of expertise and drew us together as a team; we needed each other to succeed. The rewards and frustrations of the classroom and our collaboration influenced our own research collaboration influenced our own research perspectives as well. Being in the classroom and working together "kept us honest." Despite difficulties in achieving this kind of collaborative classroom research, we all concluded that it is highly important. It costs school districts very little and has potentially significant benefits for the students, for other teachers, and for the university research community.

Teacher collaboration at the school site

Given the school structure at schools like Mayfair, there is real potential for collaboration among the teachers in each of the colleges. There are four teachers of the academic subjects (math, science, history, and English) in each college, working with the same group of students. They are in a position to design teaching strategies and interdisciplinary lessons which could stress the features that were used and were successful during this study: a non-competitive classroom structure with effort-based grading, multiple performance opportunities, increased student responsibility and choice, and the validation of cultural heritage.

This "college" structure also makes it possible for the groups of teachers in each college to develop a system by which they can each focus on a designated number of students in their college in order to become familiar with their needs, interests, and career aspirations, so that they can guide them, monitor their progress, and act as their advocates.

Along with collaborating with academics at local universities and with their own colleagues, another important kind of teacher collaboration is that between the teacher and their students.

Teacher–student collaboration in the classroom

One of the most important lessons we learned from this four-year study was how valuable our students' ideas are. Without the data we collected from student interviews and questionnaires, we would have gained much less insight into their beliefs about themselves as students, about Karen as their teacher, and about their future aspirations. This information guided Karen in the adjustments she made over the years in her efforts to better support her students. Teachers should not consider their students as merely passive recipients of knowledge they give to them.

Instead, they should see them as vibrant, intelligent, thoughtful young people whose ideas and reactions to classroom experiences can contribute enormously to teachers' own personal growth and development in their profession.

All these implications for teaching and for collaboration – between schools and universities, on the school site, and between teachers and their students – should be introduced and explored in teacher education programs as prospective teachers are introduced to key issues in the teaching profession.

Implications for teacher education

> It is possible that all of the cultures of the world might become respected in the curriculum, and that a new generation of young and romantic teachers will join with those of us who have been around for a while to reassert, in our classrooms and in the community, the idea that each and every child has unknown and unpredictable potential.
>
> (Kohl, 1967: ix)

There are a number of implications for teacher education that can be drawn from this study. First, beginning teachers should be taught various theories of achievement motivation and school failure so that they will take them into consideration in their classroom approach. Student teachers typically have classes in cognitive development, adolescent behavior, and other relatively general topics, preparing them for the kinds of personalities and variations in development they can expect to find among their students. However, the phenomenon of negative motivation, its possible causes and how to influence the students in a positive way, are rarely addressed. Student teachers need to understand how previous experiences with failure have affected their students' ways of thinking about themselves and about school, and they need to begin their teaching careers with some tools to help them work with this difficult problem.

Second, success-oriented classrooms and an understanding of how to diversify tasks should be promoted. Because most beginning teachers are products of the educational system as it is now, they have succeeded in classrooms where competition was fostered and where success was determined primarily by the completion of homework and high scores on tests. Designing a teaching approach that reduces competition and promotes student success through a variety of performance opportunities is not easy and is very hard to accomplish single-handedly. We know this from experience! Beginning teachers should be encouraged to work together during their teacher education programs and throughout their teaching careers to diversify the curriculum so that the multiple learning styles and the strengths and talents their students have will be addressed.

Third, new teachers should be exposed to different methods of incorporating cultural awareness and pride into their curriculum and have practice in doing so. Since African American students have clearly suffered in school because their own cultural heritage has been overlooked, it is vital that teachers work together to remedy this shortcoming. Studies have proven time and time again that a student's self-concept is one of the key factors for success in school. The more teachers can do to embrace all the cultures represented by their students the better their students will feel about who they are, who they were, and who they will become.

Finally, the most significant implication from this study for teacher education is the value of teacher research in preparing methods and materials, in implementing them, and in assessing their impact on the students. Unless beginning teachers think of themselves not only as curriculum developers and practitioners but also as problem-solvers through careful investigation of their own teaching, then many of these reasons for school failure will not be altered. Beginning teachers should be encouraged to become teacher researchers during their teacher education programs every time they visit a classroom – whether to teach or to observe. They then should have several opportunities during their education to discuss with others in their program teaching issues they have observed and studied. Only through those kinds of experiences will the value of collaboration and teacher research become clear.

Appendices

Appendix A: End of year group interview questions

Directions read to interviewees: This is an interview that we do with students at the end of the year to get their thoughts about the class. We do this in order to see if what we did was effective, and also to make changes for next time. That's why it's very important that you answer honestly. Your answers give us very important information. The questions come from the questionnaire you filled out last week.

1   Do you think that your grade in this class is based on different kinds of assignments?
2   Most students said that they were getting higher grades in this class. Why do you think that this is true?
3   Do you think you learn more in your other classes?
4   Why do you think we have class officers? Are there other ways students could take responsibility for the class?
5   Most students said that they felt good about being able to read books about people from their own race. What do you think?
6   Do you like how the class has had discussions about important current events? Why?
7   Give us some thoughts about everything that you think is really good about this class, that you really like, and also things that are bad about this class, compared to your other classes. Things like how the class is run, how the teachers treat you, and some of the things you would really like to change.

Appendix B: Student questionnaire

1 The harder I work in this class, the better grade I will get.
TRUE   FALSE

2 Only some people in this class can get an "A."
TRUE   FALSE

3 I don't feel comfortable sharing my ideas in this class.
TRUE   FALSE

Because:

4 In this class I have been able to improve my grade by re-doing assignments or turning them in late.
TRUE   FALSE

If you circled "False," please explain your answer:

5 Are you getting a better grade in this class than in most of your other classes?
YES   NO

If you are getting a better grade in this class, list as many reasons for this as you can think of below:

6 How do you feel about having choices in the books you read and on some of your assignments?

7 Do you think it's a good idea to have classroom officers?
YES   NO

Why or why not?

8 Do you have class officers in your other classes?
YES   NO

9 How do you feel about being able to read books about people from your own race?

Appendix C: Questionnaire about grades

1   At the beginning of the quarter, what grade did you want in this class?
    A   B   C   D   F
2   *Now*, with the quarter over, what grade did you actually get in this class on your report card?
    A   B   C   D   F

Why?

3   What would be a good grade for you in this class? (You can circle more than one grade.)
    A   B   C   D   F
4   What is the lowest grade you can get in this class and still be proud of your grade?
    A   B   C   D   F

Why – what makes you proud of a grade?

5   What grade does your parent or guardian expect in this class?
    A   B   C   D   F
6   What is the lowest grade you can get in this class and still stay out of trouble with your parent or guardian?
    A   B   C   D   F
7   Are you getting a higher grade in this class than in your other classes?
    YES   NO

If yes, give 3 reasons why:

(1)

(2)

(3)

8   What other thoughts do you have about this class?

Appendix D: Questionnaire about interests

1   Check the school-connected skills you *like the best*:

reading	organizing (binder/homework)	building
writing	being a leader	games
spelling	singing	problem solving
speaking	dancing	drawing
map work	answering questions from the book	
others?		

2   Check the school-connected skills you *want/need to improve on*:

reading	organizing (binder/homework)	building
writing	being a leader	games
spelling	singing	problem solving
speaking	dancing	map work
answering questions from the book	drawing	
others?		

3   Check your interests *outside of school*:

reading	movies	exercise
sports	puzzles	music
parties	cards	friends
drawing	biking	building models
TV	games	shopping
others?		

4   List the *careers* you might be interested in as an adult:

5   What *colleges or universities* are you interested in?

Bibliography

Anderson, G., Herr, K., and Nihlen, A. (1994) *Studying your own school.* Thousand Oaks, CA: Corwin Press.

Anyon, J. (1981) Social class and school knowledge. *Curriculum Inquiry*, 11(1): 3–42.

Bennet, C. (1985) Paints, pots or promotion? Art teachers' attitudes towards their careers. In S. Ball and I. Goodson (eds) *Teachers' lives and careers*, pp. 120–37. London: The Falmer Press.

Bernstein, B. (1977) Social class, language, and socialization. In J. Karabel and A.H. Halsey (eds) *Power and ideology in education*. New York: Oxford University Press.

Boateng, F. (1990) Combating deculturalization of the African American child in the public school system: a multi-cultural approach. In K. Lomotey (ed.) *Going to school: The African-American experience*, pp. 73–84. Albany: State University of New York Press.

Bourdieu, P. (1977) Cultural reproduction and social reproduction. In J. Karabel and A.H. Halsey (eds) *Power and ideology in education*. New York: Oxford University Press.

Bowles, S. and Gintis, H. (1986) *Schooling in capitalist America.* New York: Basic Books.

Boykin, A.W. (1994) Afrocultural expression and its implications for schooling. In E.R. Hollins, J.E. King, and W.C. Hayman (eds) *Teaching diverse populations: formulating a knowledge base*, pp. 243–56. New York: State University of New York Press.

Brophy, J.E. (1987) Synthesis of research on strategies for motivating students to learn. *Educational Leadership*, 45(2): 40–8.

Bullough, J.R. Jr. and Gitlin, A. (1995) *Becoming a student of teaching.* New York: Garland Publishing, Inc.

Carter, P. (1999, March) What's school got to do with it? Further explanation of the attitude achievement paradox among low-income minority adolescents. Paper presented at the annual meeting of the American Educational Research Association, Montreal, Canada.

Clark, A.N. (1976) *Secret of the Andes.* New York: Viking Press.

Cochran-Smith, M. and Lytle, S. (1990) Research on teaching and teacher research: the issues that divide. *Educational Researcher*, 19(2): 2–11.

—— (1993) *Inside/outside: teacher research and knowledge*. New York: Teachers College Press.

Coleman, J. (1966) *Equality of educational opportunity*. Washington, DC: US Printing Office.

Connelly, M.F. and Clandinin, J.D. (1987) On narrative method: biography and narrative unities in the study of teaching. *Journal of Educational Thought*, 21(3): 130–9.

—— (1990) Stories of experience and narrative inquiry. *Educational Researcher*, 19(4): 2–13.

Covington, M.V. (1984) The self-worth theory of achievement motivation: findings and implications. *Elementary School Journal*, 85(1): 5–20.

—— (1992) *Making the grade: a self-worth perspective on motivation and school reform*. New York: Cambridge University Press.

—— (1998) *The will to learn: a guide for motivating young people*. New York: Cambridge University Press.

Covington, M.V. and Beery, R.G. (1976) *Self-worth theory and school learning*. New York: Holt, Rinehart and Winston.

Covington, M.V. and Omelich, C.L. (1979) Effort: the double-edged sword in school achievement. *Journal of Educational Psychology*, 71(2): 169–82.

Covington, M.V. and Teel, K.M. (1996) *Overcoming student failure: changing motives and incentives for learning*. Washington, DC: American Psychological Association.

Cummins, J. (1986) Empowering minority students: a framework for intervention. *Harvard Educational Review*, 56(1): 18–36.

Delpit, L.D. (1988) The silenced dialogue: power and pedagogy in educating other people's children. *Harvard Educational Review*, 58(3): 280–98.

—— (1995) *Other people's children: conflict in the classroom*. New York: New Press.

Diller, D. (1999) Opening the dialogue: using culture as a tool in teaching young African American children. *The Reading Teacher*, 52(8) (May): 820–8.

Edmonds, R. (1978, July) A discussion of the literature and issues related to effective schooling. Paper presented at the National Conference on Urban Education. St. Louis, Missouri.

Fordham, S. and Ogbu, J.U. (1986) Black students' school success: coping with the "burden of 'acting white'." *Urban Review*, 18(3): 176–206.

Friend, R.M. and Neale, J.M. (1972) Children's perceptions of success and failure: an attributional analysis of the effects of race and social class. *Developmental Psychology*, 7: 124–8.

Giroux, H. (1983) *Theory and resistance in education*. London: Heinemann Educational Books.

—— (1984) Public philosophy and the crisis of education. *Harvard Educational Review*, 54(2): 186–95.

Glaser, B. and Strauss, A. (1967) *The discovery of grounded theory: strategies for qualitative research*. New York: Aldine De Gruyter.

Graham, S. (1988) Can attribution theory tell us something about motivation in Blacks? *Educational Psychologist*, 23(1): 3–21.

—— (1994) Motivation in African-Americans. *Review of Educational Research*, 64(1): 55–118.

Haberman, M. (1991) The pedagogy of poverty versus good teaching. *Phi Delta Kappan*, 73(4): 290–4.

Hale, J.E. (1994) *Unbank the fire: visions for the education of African American children*. Baltimore, MD: Johns Hopkins University Press.

Hale-Benson, J. (1990) Visions for children: educating black children in the context of their culture. In K. Lomotey (ed.) *Going to school: the African-American experience*, pp. 209–22. Albany: State University of New York Press.

Heath, S.B. (1983) *Ways with words: language, life, and work in communities and classrooms*. New York: Cambridge University Press.

—— (1986) What no bedtime story means: narrative skills at home and at school. In B.B. Schieffelin and E. Ochs (eds) *Language socialization across cultures*, pp. 97–124. New York: Cambridge University Press.

Hilliard, A. (1978) Equal educational opportunity and quality education. *Anthropology and Education Quarterly*, 9: 110–26.

Hollingsworth, S., Cody, A., Davis-Smallwood, J., Dybdahl, M., Gallagher, P., Gallego, M., Maestre, T., Minarik, L., Raffel, L., Standerford, N.S., and Teel, K. (1994) *Teacher research and urban literacy education*. New York: Teachers College Press.

Hollingsworth, S., Teel, K., and Minarik, L. (1992) Learning to teach Aaron: a beginning teacher's story of literacy instruction in an urban classroom. *Journal of Teacher Education*, 43(2): 116–27.

Howe, K. (1992) Liberal democracy, equal educational opportunity, and the challenge of multiculturalism. *American Educational Research Journal*, 29(3): 455–70.

Irvine, J. (1990) *Black students and school failure: policies, practices and prescriptions*. New York: Greenwood Press.

Jencks, C., Smith, M., Acland, H., Bane, M.J., Cohen, D., Gintis, H., Heyns, B., and Michelson, S.(1972) *Inequality: a reassessment of the effect of family and schooling in America*. New York: Basic Books.

Knapp, M.S., Shields, P.M., and Turnbull, P.M. (1992) *Academic challenges for the children of poverty: summary report*. Washington, DC: US Department of Education.

Kohl, H. (1967) *36 children*. New York: Penguin Books.

Ladson-Billings, G. (1994) *The dreamkeepers: successful teachers of African-American children*. San Francisco: Jossey Bass.

Lampert, M. (1991) Knowing and telling about teaching: paradoxes and problems in being a school teacher and a university researcher. Paper presented at the annual meeting of the American Educational Research Association, Chicago, Illinois.

Leondari, A., Syngollitou, E., and Kiosseoglou, G. (1998) Academic achievement, motivation and possible selves. *Journal of Adolescence*, 21: 219–22.

Lomotey, K. (1990) Introduction. In K. Lomotey (ed.) *Going to school: the African-American experience*, pp. 1–9. Albany: State University of New York Press.

Lortie, D. (1975) *Schoolteacher: a sociological study*. Chicago: University of Chicago Press.

MacLeod, J. (1987) *Ain't no makin' it: leveled aspirations in a low-income neighborhood*. Boulder, CO: Westview Press.

Marchant, G.J. (1990) Intrinsic motivation, self-perception, and their effects on black urban elementary students. Paper presented at the annual meeting of the American Educational Research Association, Boston, MA.

Marshall, H.H. and Weinstein, R.S. (1984) Classroom factors affecting students' self-evaluations: an interactional model. *Review of Educational Research*, 54(3): 301–25.

—— (1986) Classroom context of student-perceived differential teacher treatment. *Journal of Educational Psychology*, 78(6), 441–53.

Mickelson, R. (1990) The attitude-achievement paradox among Black adolescents. *Sociology of Education*, 63(1): 44–61.

Miles, M.B. and Huberman, A.M. (1984) *Qualitative data analysis: a sourcebook of new methods*. Beverly Hills, CA: Sage.

Mills, G.E. (2000) *Action research*. New Jersey: Prentice-Hall, Inc.

Nieto, S. (1999) *The light in their eyes: creating intercultural learning communities*. New York: Teachers College Press.

Oakes, J. (1985) *Keeping track: how schools structure inequality*. New Haven, CT: Yale University Press.

Obidah, J. and Teel, K.M. (1996) The impact of race and cultural differences on the teacher/student relationship: a collaborative classroom study by an African American and a Caucasian teacher research team. *Kansas Association for Supervision and Curriculum Development*, 14(1): 70–80.

—— (2001) *Because of the kids: facing racial and cultural differences in schools*. New York: Teachers College Press.

Ogbu, J. (1987) Opportunity structure, cultural boundaries, and literacy. In Judith Langer (ed.) *Language, literacy, and culture: issues of society and schooling*. Norwood, NJ: Ablex.

—— (1990) Literacy and schooling in subordinate cultures: the case of Black Americans. In K. Lomotey (ed.) *Going to school: the African American experience*, pp. 113–31. Albany: State University of New York Press.

—— (1994) Racial stratification in the United States: why inequality persists. *Teachers College Record*, 96(2): 264–98.

Ogbu, J. and Matute-Bianchi, M. (1986) Understanding sociocultural factors: knowledge, identity, and school adjustment. In *Beyond language: social and cultural factors in schooling language minority students*, pp. 74–142. Los Angeles: California State University.

Ossie, D. (1978) *Escape to freedom*. New York: Viking Press.

Phillips, S.U. (1972) Participant structures and communicative competence: Warm Springs children in community and classroom. In C.B. Cazden, V.P. John, and D. Hymes (eds) *Functions of language in the classroom*, pp. 370–94. New York: Teachers College Press.

Rashid, H.M. (1981) Early childhood education as a cultural transition for African American children. *Educational Research Quarterly*, 6(3): 55–63.

Rosenholtz, S.J. (1979) The classroom equalizer. *Teacher*, 97(1): 78–9.

Rosenholtz, S.J. and Simpson, C. (1984) The formation of ability conceptions: developmental trend or social construction. *Review of Educational Research*, 54(1): 31–63.

Rubin, L.(1976) *Worlds of pain: life in the working-class family.* New York: Basic Books.

Sleeter, C. (1994) White racism. *Multicultural Education*, 1(9): 5–8, 39.

Teel, K.M., Covington, M.V., and DeBruin-Parecki, A. (1994) Promoting and sustaining a shift in motivation among "low-achieving" African American middle school students: a praxiological educology. *International Journal of Educology*, 8(2): 138–51.

Teel, K.M., DeBruin-Parecki, A., and Covington, M.V. (1998) Teaching strategies that honor and motivate inner-city African American students: a school–university collaboration. *Teaching and Teacher Education*, 14(5); 479–95.

Thomas, J.W. (1980) Agency and achievement: self-management and self-regard. *Review of Educational Research*, 50(2): 213–40.

US Census and Bureau of Labor Statistics, compiled by the National Council of La Raza, 1997.

Verble, M. (1985) How to encourage self-discipline. *Learning*, 14(1): 40–3.

Weiner, B. (1972) *Theories of motivation: from mechanism to cognition.* Chicago: Markham.

—— (1977) An attribution model for educational psychology. In L. Shulman (ed.) *Review of research in education*, vol. 4. Itasca, IL: Peacock.

Weinstein, R.S. (1983) Student perceptions of schooling. *Elementary School Journal*, 83(4): 289–312.

—— (1986) The teaching of reading and children's awareness of teacher expectations. In T. Raphael (ed.) *The contexts of school-based literacy*, pp. 233–52. New York: Random House.

—— (1989) Perception of classroom processes and student motivation: children's views of self-fulfilling prophecies. In R.E. Ames and C. Ames (eds) *Research on motivation in education*, vol. 3. New York: Academic Press.

—— (1991) Expectations and high school change: teacher–researcher collaborations to prevent school failure. *American Journal of Community Psychology*, 19(3): 333–63.

Weinstein, R.S., Marshall, H.H., Brattesani, K.A., and Middlestadt, S.E. (1982) Student perceptions of differential teacher treatment in open and traditional classrooms. *Journal of Educational Psychology*, 74(4): 678–92.

Index

59; school failure 17, 18;
students' strengths 21; teacher
expectation 11, 19;
underachievement 12

work sessions, extra 81–2;
assignments 85–9; impact
93–4

World History 32–3